AF729834

AI AT WORK

AI AT WORK

How to build a full stack organization

JAMES POULTER

BLOOMSBURY BUSINESS
LONDON • NEW YORK • OXFORD • NEW DELHI • SYDNEY

BLOOMSBURY BUSINESS
Bloomsbury Publishing Plc, 50 Bedford Square, London, WC1B 3DP, UK
Bloomsbury Publishing Inc, 1359 Broadway, New York, NY 10018, USA
Bloomsbury Publishing Ireland Limited, 29 Earlsfort Terrace, Dublin 2, D02 AY28, Ireland

BLOOMSBURY, BLOOMSBURY BUSINESS and the Diana logo are trademarks of Bloomsbury Publishing Plc

First published in Great Britain 2026

Copyright © James Poulter, 2026

James Poulter has asserted his right under the Copyright, Designs and Patents Act, 1988, to be identified as Author of this work.

For legal purposes the Acknowledgements on p. vi constitute an extension of this copyright page.

Cover design: Louise Dugdale

All rights reserved. No part of this publication may be: i) reproduced or transmitted in any form, electronic or mechanical, including photocopying, recording or by means of any information storage or retrieval system without prior permission in writing from the publishers; or ii) used or reproduced in any way for the training, development or operation of artificial intelligence (AI) technologies, including generative AI technologies. The rights holders expressly reserve this publication from the text and data mining exception as per Article 4(3) of the Digital Single Market Directive (EU) 2019/790.

Bloomsbury Publishing Plc does not have any control over, or responsibility for, any third-party websites referred to or in this book. All internet addresses given in this book were correct at the time of going to press. The author and publisher regret any inconvenience caused if addresses have changed or sites have ceased to exist, but can accept no responsibility for any such changes.

A catalogue record for this book is available from the British Library.

ISBN: HB: 978-1-3505-9792-1
ePDF: 978-1-3505-9790-7
ePub: 978-1-3505-9791-4

Typeset by RefineCatch Limited, Bungay, Suffolk
Printed and bound in Great Britain

For product safety related questions contact productsafety@bloomsbury.com.

To find out more about our authors and books visit www.bloomsbury.com and sign up for our newsletters.

CONTENTS

ACKNOWLEDGEMENTS

The writing of this book came as a direct result of seeing the impact AI was having – and going to have – on the publishing industry. It emerged from engagement with my client, now publisher, Bloomsbury, who subsequently asked me to write this book for all of you to read. So if I have to begin an acknowledgements section somewhere, it's best to start there – and in particular with my fantastic editor Alex Davies, thank you for all your feedback and help getting this to market.

Once it became clear that this work was necessary, the world has continued to adopt AI both hastily and, in many cases, scarily. But as I have gone about my work, I find in rooms all over the world that there continues to be a great need for thoughtful, ethical adoption of AI. Along the way, several people have helped sharpen my thinking on these subjects, and I would like to acknowledge them here.

Thanks must go to my fellow AI enthusiasts and scholars: Joshua Seale, Dr Stuart Cranney, Patricia Shaw, David Brenner, Dr Michael Arena, Dr John Lennox, and Dr John Dyer have all – directly and through their writings – influenced my thinking on the future of AI and the ethics of its adoption. Thanks also to my friends and collaborators Peter Erickson and Emerson Sklar for making space for me to share my views with the AI industry.

To my colleagues at Elvis – Phil Fearnley and Lucy Freedman, my co-founder Jen Heape, and my fantastic assistant Jemma Kaczmarska: thank you for giving me the space to work on this project and keeping me on track.

To my fantastic agents Matthew Fisher, Jessica Lalley and Julie Shaffner: thank you for all the discussions, stages, flights and networks you have unlocked for me, helping more people hear these thoughts and messages.

To my parents and siblings – Martin, Lesley, Jan, Alex, Daniel and Ellie – thank you for your constant encouragement and support, without which this book would not have come to be. And to Simon, for inspiring my career in communications: you are always with us.

To my darling wife Holly, and my girls Hazel and Willow: I'm sorry for every missed bedtime this project has taken away, but thank you for always being there for me, for understanding my mission, supporting my passion, and carrying me through every twist. You are my rocks.

And to you, dear reader: thank you for letting me speak into your work. I hope these thoughts, stories, and perspectives bless what you do – the work to which God calls each of us uniquely.

I am glad this calling is mine.

Introduction: From FOMO to FOJO

I got my first job at fifteen. My National Insurance card hadn't arrived yet – or was still in the post – so if anyone from HMRC is reading, go gently. I worked at a dry cleaning company in southwest London in a decidedly well-to-do area. For British readers, the Waitrose on the high street tells you everything you need to know about the neighbourhood.

Surrounded by clingfilm-wrapped jackets and blouses, amid the smell of cleaning products and the occasional ring of the doorbell announcing customers, I'd spend my shifts thinking about my media studies coursework due at the end of the week while shrouding garments in protective film.

We had some notable customers – including Kate Winslet, the BAFTA and Oscar-winning actress, whose ball gowns were regularly dropped off (though I never saw her in person). Occasionally, we'd also handle suits belonging to Sir Cliff Richard himself. It's worth noting I never met, nor saw any of these celebrity clients, but my boss Michael (not his real name for above cash-in-hand-based reasons) assured me they were legit.

After a summer slinging jackets, I got upgraded to slinging papers as I shuttled legal documents from my father's barrister's chambers up and down Fleet Street in Central London. He was a senior clerk to one of the premium sets in London's busy Lincoln's Inn, the home of the legal world in the centre of the bustling city.

These boxes of papers were housed in cardboard containers wrapped with a thin pink ribbon – a sight all barristers and clerks of that era would recognize and which can still occasionally be seen today.[1] This was the Dropbox of 1998, the Gmail of the 1990s – information moving at whatever speed I could lug a carton of papers up and down the stairs of the leather-padded, mahogany-clad offices of Her Majesty's Queen's Counsel.

It's fair to say work has come on a long way since then, and certainly the way we move information. These jobs now seem almost quaint in their simplicity. Yet they illustrate something profound about how work has fundamentally transformed in just a few decades, and help us understand why we're standing at such a critical inflection point with artificial intelligence.

While jobs like these still exist today, many similar roles have disappeared due to automation. I believe these two particular jobs are relatively AI-proof, but much of the drudgery associated with this type of work sits on the edge of being automated away – and that's precisely what this book will help you navigate.

If you're leading an organization of any kind – whether it's an entrepreneurial start-up, a large enterprise, a division of a multinational, a community group or church, a charitable organization, or simply trying to lead your household effectively – you face one fundamental challenge: how do you lead in the age of AI?

The great job fragmentation

A recent browse through LinkedIn reveals engineering roles that have exploded into dozens of specialized positions[2] – artificial intelligence engineer, back-end

---

[1]One day the courts will get AI, but that's for another time.

[2]LinkedIn Economic Graph (2023) 'The changing world of work: job titles and skills trends'. Available at: https://economicgraph.linkedin.com

software engineer, data scientist, machine learning engineer – roles that were once simply 'engineer'. McKinsey data shows that Fortune 500 companies have seen a 37 per cent increase in job titles in just the twenty years since the mid-2000s.[3] It's got almost comically out of hand, job titles now read like superhero alter egos:

Change Chatter

Retail Jedi

Accounting Ninja

We've fragmented work into smaller and smaller bite-sized chunks, created deep specializations for each fragment, then stratified them through junior, mid-weight, senior and executive levels. Somewhere in that stack, we've all become more broken into different parts of what we do.

This fragmentation wasn't random – it all traces back to putting computers on our desks. That single change catalysed a series of macro trends that nobody predicted when the computer first came into the office:

- Technological complexity crept in, forcing us into our own systems, silos, and ways of doing things.
- Process fragmentation broke our tasks down into smaller parts so we could give people different jobs to own different pieces.
- Deep specialization became necessary as each fragment required specific expertise.
- Scaling challenges emerged because, to make organizations bigger, we had to fragment processes down and replicate them over and over again.

---

[3]McKinsey & Company (2024) 'Generative AI and the future of work: job fragmentation and new roles'. www.mckinsey.com

And technology just made this ultimately more complicated.

Understanding this fragmentation is crucial because we're now seeing it begin to reverse. Recent data shows we're already seeing 31 per cent fewer specialized roles being hired for in some sectors.[4] The specialization of jobs is beginning to 'frazzle at the edges' because AI systems can be trained on specialist knowledge, meaning humans need to become more capable of doing the stuff that AIs can't do well.

For most of us in the knowledge economy – those whose jobs would be very hard to do without a computer – this transformation is already underway. If you spend your days moving bits and information around, either from person to person or organization to organization, whether in legal services, HR, education or countless other sectors, then AI is going to impact what you do to a greater or lesser extent.

Walk into any average business and you'll see people sitting behind computers: sending emails, doing research, organizing documents, creating documents, sending more emails. All of these activities – relating with other humans, sending information, creating documents – are fundamentally about to change in terms of what it means to do that type of work.

The rise of the full stack professional

But this shift isn't just about job displacement – it's about fundamental role transformation. We're moving towards what I call the 'full stack professional'. When we stop fragmenting different roles into different parts, and we begin to have to do all of it a bit more because we've got AIs to help us, we start modelling a new form of professionalism.

[4]www.mckinsey.com/uk/our-insights/the-mckinsey-uk-blog/ai-uneven-effects-on-uk-jobs-and-talent

The term 'full stack' comes from software development, where a full stack developer can work across all layers of an application – front end, back end, database, everything. Full stack professionals in the AI age will similarly work across multiple domains that were previously specialized roles, but with AI systems handling the technical execution while humans focus on orchestration, strategy and the uniquely human elements.

This represents a return to integration after decades of fragmentation. Instead of the traditional organizational pyramid with lots of junior staff gradually narrowing to more senior expertise at the top, we're seeing organizations develop into a 'diamond shape' – a much wider breadth of expertise in the centre, but fewer traditional junior roles.

The middle of organizations is about to get much bigger, filled with professionals who can:

- **Master AI orchestration**. What does it look like to have a thousand workers that can work faster than you, better than you in the niches you're not good at, working at your disposal and command? This is more like being a conductor of an orchestra than a player of an individual piano. You're not just setting the tune – you're making sure everyone is on board at the same time. And some of those 'people' are going to be people, and some are not going to be people.
- **Develop higher-order human skills**. Leadership, empathy, strategy, cultural fluency – things that AIs fundamentally aren't very good at. They don't have real-time access to the conversation happening in the corridor, or what just happened in the news this morning, or how people are feeling and the temperature of a place. We humans have that stuff, and it's what we need to teach.
- **Navigate cultural context**. Particularly in international businesses that have gone through mergers, acquisitions and team integrations, cultural fluency isn't just about language or heritage – it's about

understanding what it means to do this work here, with this particular group of people, in this moment.

- **Think strategically**. Strategy is a complex and amorphous thing, but humans are actually very good at it while AIs fundamentally aren't. AIs are mostly predicting from things they've seen before rather than navigating things they've never seen. We're much better at that kind of strategic thinking.

This shift towards full stack professionals will be more aligned to who you are as a person at core personality and value levels than the skills you accumulated through university and early career years. Think of it like the difference between Myers-Briggs profiles and job descriptions – your fundamental way of approaching problems becomes more important than your specific technical training.

So where are we now? FOMO turns to FOJO

I've been trying to summarize this for people as AI momentum has built, and I would put it this way: 2024 and the latter part of 2023 was the age of 'FOMO' when it came to AI. You know what FOMO is – Fear of Missing Out. Everybody jumping on the bandwagon, everyone looking for ways to do more of this type of stuff. 'Let's use ChatGPT, let's get Copilot, let's build our own thing.' People were creating cartoon action figures of themselves just because they could.

The fear of missing out was what catalysed most of our initial interest in trying out AI. But the reason I get booked to speak to organizations more often these days isn't because of the FOMO part – it's what I call 'FOJO': the Fear of Job Obsolescence. 'This is going to take my job.' I hear that all the time. More broadly: 'Is this going to take my job? Are bits of the economy going to become obsolete?' It breeds a form of AI anxiety. When people look at their daily and weekly schedules, they think, 'There are bits of this which an AI should be doing, rather than me sitting here doing it.'

You've probably heard the phrase: 'AI is not going to take your job – someone who knows how to use AI is going to take your job.' I used to think that was fair, but now I think it's rubbish. Some AIs are going to take some jobs, and we should just own up to that. Not be afraid of it, just accept it and decide what to do about it. Maybe not your job, but maybe the job you never chose to recruit for, or the job someone five years down the line was going to have – or not, as the case may be. The idea that AI is going to significantly impact how we work seems somewhat inevitable. And if anything is inevitable, you start preparing for it.

The AI inflection point: understanding our moment

This isn't just about individual jobs or even individual productivity gains. Recent research shows[5] that individuals with AI can match the performance of teams of three to four people who don't have access to AI. Teams given AI access are three times more likely to produce exceptional solutions – those in the top 10 per cent of quality outcomes.

When we have teams that are three times more effective and able to produce top-quality outcomes, we enter into a very different shape of work. But here's the challenge: most organizations are approaching AI as if it's just another tool to add to their existing fragmented systems. They're missing the bigger picture. We need a new kind of nervous system in the way we work. This is more than just an extension of how we work – it's rewiring it entirely.

One of the few university books I kept from my days at the University of Westminster library was Marshall McLuhan's *Understanding Media: The*

---

[5]www.library.hbs.edu/working-knowledge/when-ai-joins-the-team-better-ideas-surface

Extensions of Man.[6] McLuhan describes electric technology as being 'within the gates of the citadel' – meaning electricity is reshaping patterns of social interdependence and every aspect of our personal lives. He portrays electronic media as an extension of humanity – specifically of our nervous system – creating a 'global village' where information flows instantaneously across vast distances.

While this extension metaphor applies to AI, I believe something even more profound is happening. AI isn't just extending our capabilities – it's completely rewiring how we work. McLuhan focused on how digital media would accelerate our connections, allowing us to share knowledge across vast distances and communities.

What we're witnessing now is more like a nervous system rewiring.

Traditional work hierarchies and information flows – even how information comes into being – will no longer depend solely on how quickly humans can create and share it. Instead, all information will live in one interconnected space where we can collectively learn from and build upon it over time. This collective intelligence within our organizations presents the central challenge for leaders of AI-enabled companies – how to effectively harness, leverage, and cultivate this shared intelligence.

I think AI represents a rewiring of the circuitry of how we do work. Your organization needs more than scattered AI tools – it needs an AI nervous system. Just as your biological nervous system coordinates information flow, decision-making and responses throughout your body, an organizational AI nervous system coordinates intelligence, decision-making, and action across your enterprise.

---

[6]McLuhan, M. (1964) *Understanding Media: The Extensions of Man*. New York: McGraw-Hill.

The three parts of your AI nervous system

Every good nervous system has three parts to it, and this framework will structure our entire approach to building sustainable AI capabilities that support full stack professionals.

Part One: The brain – building better intelligence

The first part of our ecosystem is the brain. These AI models we're talking about – large language models – are more like brains than they are algorithms. You know what an algorithm is, right? A simple algorithm would be A + B = C. Whatever we put in the front end, we all get the same answer out the back. But these AI systems don't work like algorithms. They have algorithms in them, but they're much more like brains, relying on transformer technology. The brain section of this book will cover:

- **Beyond algorithms**: understanding how large language models actually work and why they're revolutionary.
- **The data challenge**: making models work for you through techniques like Retrieval Augmented Generation (RAG) – bringing your organizational knowledge to AI.
- **Infrastructure for intelligence**: the technical requirements for building an AI nervous system that integrates with your existing tech stack.

Part Two: The gut – ethical intelligence

For a long time in neuroscience, we thought the brain controlled everything in our system. But we've learned that the gut also plays a big part in managing the nervous system – things like mood, temperature and sensory awareness. This relationship is known as the gut–brain axis.

When we talk about AI, we can get very technical about the brain part and miss the point. One of the biggest things we can do to create a great AI ecosystem is think really deeply about the human part – that gut instinct. You've heard that phrase, right? 'I felt it in my gut' or 'I had a gut feeling about this.' The gut section will explore:

- **The human in the loop**: determining when humans should be in, on or out of AI decision-making.
- **Developing AI gut instinct**: building ethical frameworks into your AI approach.
- **The AI seatbelt problem**: personal and organizational responsibility for AI safety, and practical safeguards.

Part Three: The hands and feet – practical applications

The final part of our nervous system is where intention becomes action – the hands and feet. This is where AI capabilities translate into real work, real outcomes and real business value.

We're seeing the emergence of what researchers call 'vibe coding'[7] – a new form of programming where you give in to whatever the AI model does and just keep going, embracing the exponentials. This isn't happening just in code as a discipline, but across many knowledge work domains. We're witnessing the evolution from AI assistants to true AI agents that can take on tasks autonomously. The hands and feet section will cover:

- **The new work paradigm**: what work looks like when the human becomes the orchestrator.
- **Leading in the AI age:** what it means to build teams, companies and organizations in a world of AI colleagues.

---

[7]https://en.wikipedia.org/wiki/Vibe_coding

- **Building your AI adoption roadmap**: assessment frameworks, prioritization methodologies and change management approaches.

Leading AI – the task of the next decade

We're at an inflection point that's bigger than individual job displacement or productivity gains. The organizations that thrive in the next decade will be those that successfully transition from fragmented, tool-based approaches to AI towards integrated nervous systems that amplify human intelligence rather than replace it.

The choice isn't whether AI will transform your organization – it's whether you'll lead that transformation thoughtfully and intentionally, or whether it will happen to you in ways you don't control. This book is your guide to making that choice deliberately.

I'll take you through building each part of your AI nervous system, from understanding the technical foundations in the brain, to developing ethical frameworks in the gut, to implementing practical applications through the hands and feet. By the end, you'll have a complete roadmap for building sustainable AI capabilities that serve your organization's values and amplify human potential. Whether you're leading a business (large or small), a community or faith group, or an educational institution, the principles apply.

The journey from FOMO to FOJO doesn't have to end in obsolescence anxiety. With the right nervous system approach, it can lead to organizational intelligence that's more human, more effective and more aligned with your deepest values and highest aspirations. But first, in order for us to be able to understand how to become the leaders that we need, who can implement this new nervous system, we have to look at how AI change happens at the three levels of leadership – personal, corporate and societal.

Key takeaways

- Fragmentation is giving way to orchestration – the 'AI nervous system' frames how to lead the shift.
- Full stack professionals will anchor the wider middle of organizations.
- FOJO is real, but preparation beats panic, and principles and practice reduce anxiety.
- Your job is to design how humans and AIs work together, not bolt tools onto old processes.

Questions for reflection

1. Where in your organization does orchestration already exist informally? How can you formalize it?
2. What fears about job change are most present on your team? How will you address them directly?
3. Which part of the nervous system should you build first – brain, gut or hands and feet? Why?
4. What would a 'diamond-shaped' team look like for you in a year?
5. What one decision this week could move you from FOMO or FOJO to forward motion?

PART ONE

THE BRAIN

1

Beyond algorithms – understanding large language models

The universal library: a thought experiment

Imagine you've been given access to a vast, extraordinary library. This isn't just any library – it contains nearly everything humanity has written: books spanning centuries, academic papers from every field, magazines, newspapers, websites, forum discussions, code repositories, instruction manuals and countless other texts. Billions of documents in hundreds of languages, all meticulously organized and accessible.

You enter this library with a question: 'What strategies helped Apple become the world's most valuable company?'

A librarian – remarkably knowledgeable but bound by certain constraints – offers to help. This librarian has read everything in the library, remembering patterns, connections, and contexts across all those texts. When you ask your question, the librarian doesn't simply point you to a single book on Apple's history. Instead, they synthesize information from business case studies, Steve Jobs biographies, financial analyses, technological histories, design philosophies and marketing textbooks to create a comprehensive answer tailored specifically to your question.

The answer isn't a collection of quotes – it's a coherent synthesis that integrates diverse perspectives into something new, yet grounded in the library's contents. The librarian can even adapt the response to your preferences: 'Give me the detailed version', you might say, or 'Explain it as if I'm a ten-year-old', and the response transforms accordingly.

This library and its librarian are remarkable, but they have limitations. First, the library stopped acquiring new materials in October 2023. Ask about events after that date, and the librarian can only speculate based on patterns observed in older materials.

Second, the librarian has no personal notes about you. If you've written a private journal or company documents that aren't in the library's collection, the librarian can't access that information. Now, imagine three upgrades to this system.

Upgrade 1: Add a computer

The library installs computers with internet access. Now when you ask about recent events – 'Who won the 2024 presidential election?' – the librarian can search online, find reliable sources and provide current information. The library is no longer frozen in time.

Upgrade 2: Add your personal notes

You're allowed to bring in your personal notebooks, journals and company documents. The librarian can now read and incorporate this private information when answering your questions. 'What did my team conclude in last week's strategy meeting?' suddenly becomes answerable.

Upgrade 3: Add memory of your conversations

The librarian begins remembering previous conversations with you, building context over time. The system becomes personalized – the librarian learns your preferences, interests and needs, making each interaction more relevant.

This thought experiment illustrates the fundamental components of modern AI systems based on large language models:

- The base library represents the pre-trained knowledge in large language models like those found in ChatGPT or Claude.
- The librarian's ability to synthesize information mirrors how these models generate text.
- The knowledge cut-off limitation reflects how models are trained on data available only up to a certain date.
- The computer upgrade represents web access capabilities.
- The personal notes upgrade illustrates Retrieval Augmented Generation (RAG).
- The conversation memory represents context retention in AI interactions.

Throughout this chapter, we'll explore how these components work together to create AI systems that can serve as the 'brain' of your organization's AI nervous system. We'll examine both their remarkable capabilities and inherent limitations – and, most importantly, how to harness them effectively.

The paradigm shift

In early 2023, I was giving a presentation to a room full of publishing executives when something remarkable happened. I asked the audience a simple question:

'What AI tools are you currently using in your daily life?' The flood of responses was immediate – ChatGPT, Claude, Gemini, various image generators, and several tools I hadn't even heard of. Almost everyone had an answer.

Just twelve months earlier, that same question would have been met with awkward silence or perhaps a handful of tentative responses about Siri or Alexa. What changed wasn't just the availability of these tools, but something far more fundamental – the emergence of a new paradigm of artificial intelligence that behaves less like the algorithms we've known for decades and more like the human brain itself.

This chapter will explore why large language models represent a fundamental shift in how we think about artificial intelligence – and why understanding this shift is crucial for any organization hoping to implement AI effectively.

The algorithm vs the brain

To understand why today's AI represents such a dramatic departure from previous technologies, we need to first understand the difference between algorithms and large language models.

Most of us interact with algorithms daily, even if we don't realize it. When you use a calculator to multiply two numbers, you're using an algorithm – a fixed set of steps that, given the same input, will always produce the same output. If I put '4 × 5' into a calculator, it will always return '20', regardless of who's using it or what calculations came before. Traditional algorithms are:

- predictable;
- rule-based;
- deterministic;
- narrow in application; and
- transparent in operation.

Consider this simple algorithm:

a + b = c

No matter what values we assign to a and b, we can predict with perfect certainty what c will be. Similarly, Einstein's famous equation $E=mc^2$ is an algorithm – plug in the values, follow the steps, and you'll get the answer.

But large language models like those in ChatGPT, Claude or Gemini operate on fundamentally different principles. They're not following predetermined steps to arrive at a single 'correct' answer. Instead, they're making probabilistic predictions based on patterns they've observed in vast amounts of text data.

When I ask ChatGPT to 'write a poem about autumn', it doesn't follow a set algorithm for poem-writing. It predicts, token by token, what words would likely follow in human-written text about autumn poems. Each word influences the probability distribution of the next word, creating a cascading effect that results in unique outputs each time. This predictive capability explains why these models can:

- generate creative content;
- adapt to context;
- understand nuance;
- generalize across domains; and
- express uncertainty.

It also explains why they can sometimes produce unexpected, inconsistent or factually incorrect responses – attributes that would be impossible with traditional algorithms.

The transformative technology – transformers

The technology enabling this revolutionary approach is the transformer architecture – the 'T' in 'GPT' (Generative Pre-trained Transformer). Developed in 2017 by researchers at Google, the transformer architecture introduced a mechanism called 'attention' that allows these models to weigh the relevance of different parts of the input when generating each part of the output.

Before transformers, AI systems struggled with understanding context over longer sequences of text. For example, in the sentence 'The trophy wouldn't fit in the suitcase because it was too big', earlier systems might have difficulty determining whether 'it' refers to the trophy or the suitcase. The transformer's attention mechanism allows it to 'focus' on relevant parts of the input text when making predictions.

Think of it like this: when you read a complex paragraph, your brain doesn't give equal weight to every word. Some words carry more meaning than others, and your understanding of later parts of the text is influenced by what came before. Transformers mimic this ability by learning which parts of the input should influence each part of the output. This seemingly technical distinction has profound implications. It means these systems can:

1. **Process language bi-directionally** – understanding context from both before and after a given word.
2. **Handle much longer sequences of text** – maintaining coherence across paragraphs or pages.
3. **Transfer learning across domains** – applying knowledge from one context to another.
4. **Generate remarkably human-like text** – with nuance, style and contextual awareness.

Perhaps most importantly, transformers can be pre-trained on massive datasets without human supervision, then fine-tuned for specific applications with much smaller amounts of labelled data. This is what made the current AI revolution economically viable.

The language model inside your head

To understand why large language models (LLMs) can seem so eerily human, it helps to recognize that you already have a language model running inside your own brain. Let's try a simple experiment. Complete this phrase:

Jack and Jill went up the . . .

If you thought 'hill', congratulations – your brain's language model just made a prediction based on patterns you've observed throughout your life. From nursery rhymes read to you as a child to cultural references you've encountered, your brain has built a statistical model of language that lets you predict what words are likely to come next in a sequence.

Your brain doesn't consciously calculate the probability of each possible next word. It seems to happen automatically, drawing on patterns you've internalized through years of language exposure. Similarly, large language models don't 'think' about what word should come next – they calculate probability distributions over their entire vocabulary and sample from those distributions.

The key difference is scale. While your language model was trained on everything you've ever read, heard or written – impressive by human standards – modern LLMs train on trillions of words from books, articles, websites, code and conversations. This allows them to develop statistical patterns for language use across virtually every domain of human knowledge represented in text. This is why these models can sometimes seem to 'know' things they were never explicitly taught. They don't have discrete facts stored in a database – they have probabilistic patterns that allow them to reconstruct information when prompted appropriately.

The library without a computer

Despite their impressive capabilities, large language models have significant limitations. I often use this analogy: interacting with a base large language model is like walking into a library with no computers.

In this library, you can access any book on the shelves, combine information from different sources, and synthesize new insights based on what's available. But you can't access anything that isn't already in the library. If you want yesterday's news or information about events that occurred after the library's collection was assembled, you're out of luck.

This is exactly the situation with large language models. They were trained on data available up to their 'knowledge cut-off date', and they have no built-in mechanism to access new information. If you ask ChatGPT about the 2024 Olympics without giving it web access, it can only make educated guesses based on patterns in its training data – it has no actual knowledge of those events. This limitation creates three challenges for organizations:

1. **Currency** – models quickly become outdated without access to recent information.
2. **Specificity** – they lack knowledge about your organization's proprietary information.
3. **Verification** – they can't independently fact-check their outputs against authoritative sources.

Fortunately, these limitations can be addressed by enhancing the 'brain' of your AI nervous system in two key ways – web access and Retrieval Augmented Generation.

Expanding the brain: web access

Adding web search capabilities to large language models is like putting a computer inside our library analogy. Suddenly, the model can reach beyond its training data to access current information, verify facts and provide more timely responses. This capability dramatically enhances what these models can do. For example, a standard language model might be able to explain the general concept of quarterly earnings reports, but with web access, it could pull up your company's most recent earnings and analyse trends against competitors.

Web access transforms language models from static repositories of past knowledge to dynamic systems that can:

- Stay current with rapidly changing information;
- verify claims against authoritative sources;
- provide evidence-based responses;
- access specialized knowledge beyond their training data; and
- compare historical patterns with current developments.

This capability is now available in many commercial AI systems, but it comes with its own challenges. The information on the web varies wildly in quality, reliability and bias. Without careful implementation, web-connected models may:

- amplify misinformation;
- present opinions as facts;
- over-rely on highly ranked but not necessarily authoritative sources;
- struggle with paywalled or access-restricted content; and
- fail to properly attribute information sources.

For organizations implementing AI, thoughtfully designed web access protocols are essential – determining which sources to prioritize, how to verify conflicting information and how to maintain transparency about information provenance.

Your notes in your notebook – Retrieval Augmented Generation

While web access solves the currency problem, it doesn't address the challenge of proprietary organizational knowledge. To return to our library analogy, what about the notes in your notebook that you just wrote during today's lecture? They're not in the library's collection, and they're not on the internet. They're unique to you.

Organizations face a similar challenge. Your internal documents, data, policies, product information, and institutional knowledge aren't readily available on the web, yet they're often the most valuable information for your specific AI use cases. This is where Retrieval Augmented Generation (RAG) comes in. RAG combines the generative capabilities of large language models with retrieval systems that can access your organization's private data stores. Here's how it works:

1. **Indexing** – your organization's documents, databases and knowledge resources are processed and indexed.
2. **Retrieval** – when a user asks a question, the system retrieves the most relevant documents or information.
3. **Augmentation** – the retrieved information is provided to the language model as additional context.
4. **Generation** – the model generates a response based on both its pre-trained knowledge and the retrieved information.

By implementing RAG, you can create AI systems that:

- answer questions about your specific products, policies or procedures;
- generate content that matches your brand voice and guidelines;
- make recommendations based on your proprietary data;
- create documentation that reflects your organization's unique processes; and
- support employees with organization-specific knowledge.

For example, a publishing company might implement a RAG system that can access its entire catalogue, contracts database, editorial guidelines and marketing materials. When an editor asks, 'What similar books have we published in the last three years that target the same audience as Project X?' the system can search internal databases, analyse similarities and generate a comprehensive response that would be impossible for a standard language model.

Building your organization's AI brain

Now that we understand the fundamental components – language models, web access and RAG – we can discuss how to build an effective AI 'brain' for your organization. The first step is to recognize that one-size-fits-all solutions rarely work. Your organization's AI brain should be designed with your specific needs, data landscape and use cases in mind. Here are the key considerations.

1. Model selection

Not all language models are created equal. They vary in:

- size and capability;
- training data;

- specialization;
- cost efficiency; and
- security and compliance features.

For many organizations, the best approach is to use different models for different purposes. You might use a powerful model like GPT 5 or Claude 4 for complex reasoning tasks while employing smaller, more efficient models for routine classification or summarization tasks.

2. Knowledge architecture

Your AI brain needs a well-organized knowledge architecture. This includes:

- Document processing pipelines – systems to convert various formats (PDFs, images, audio) into machine-readable text.
- Knowledge graphs – structured representations of entities and relationships within your domain.
- Vector databases – systems that store and retrieve information based on semantic similarity.
- Metadata systems – additional context about your information (creation date, author, department, etc.).

The goal is to make your organization's collective knowledge accessible to AI systems in ways that preserve context, relationships and relevance.

3. Integration points

Your AI brain shouldn't exist in isolation. It needs seamless connections to:

- Existing systems – CRMs, ERPs, knowledge bases, ticket systems, etc.
- Communication channels – email, chat, collaboration tools.

- Authentication systems – to manage access and permissions.
- Data lakes and warehouses – for analytical capabilities.
- Workflow tools – to automate processes end-to-end.

Each integration point increases the brain's utility but also adds complexity and potential security considerations.

4. Feedback loops

Like human brains, AI systems improve with feedback. Implement mechanisms for:

- User feedback collection – both explicit ratings and implicit signals.
- Performance monitoring – tracking accuracy, relevance and utility.
- Continuous improvement – processes to refine and enhance capabilities over time.
- Knowledge updating – systems to refresh the AI's knowledge as your organization evolves.

5. Security and governance

Your AI brain will have access to sensitive information, making security critical:

- Access controls – determining who can interact with the system and how.
- Data protection – ensuring sensitive information isn't leaked or misused.
- Audit trails – recording interactions for compliance and security.
- Content filtering – preventing harmful or inappropriate outputs.
- Privacy safeguards – protecting personal information.

Case study: Building an editorial assistant

To illustrate these principles in action, let's consider a publishing company implementing an AI brain to support its editorial team.

Challenge

Editors spend excessive time on repetitive tasks like initial manuscript assessment, market research and competitive analysis, leaving less time for the high-value work of developing authors and refining manuscripts.

Solution

An AI brain with access to:

- The company's complete catalogue and sales history.
- Editorial guidelines and style manuals.
- Manuscript submission database.
- Market research and industry reports.
- Web access for competitive research.

Implementation

1. The team selects Claude 4.5 Sonnet as their base model for its strong text analysis capabilities.
2. They build a RAG system indexing their catalogue, guidelines and submissions.
3. They implement web access with trusted industry sources prioritized.
4. They integrate with their manuscript management system.
5. They create feedback mechanisms for editors to improve responses.

Results

- Editors receive AI-generated initial assessments of manuscripts, highlighting strengths, weaknesses and market fit.
- Comparative analyses show similar titles, performance metrics and market trends.
- Editors get AI drafted notes on manuscripts based on previous reviews.
- The system learns from editor feedback, becoming more aligned with the company's editorial vision over time.

Most importantly, the system doesn't replace editorial judgement – it augments it. Editors maintain control over acquisitions and development decisions while spending less time on research and more time on creative collaboration with authors.

Looking ahead: from foundations to applications

We've covered the foundational technologies that make up the 'brain' of your AI nervous system – the large language models, web access and retrieval augmented generation that enable context-aware intelligence. These components provide the raw capabilities upon which practical applications can be built.

In the next chapter, we'll explore how to extend these capabilities by making your AI brain even smarter with your own data. We'll examine techniques for fine-tuning, domain adaptation, and creating custom embeddings that align AI capabilities with your specific organizational context.

But before we move on, remember this key insight: the brain of your AI nervous system isn't simply a larger, faster algorithm. It's a fundamentally different approach to computing that mimics aspects of human cognition through pattern recognition and prediction. By understanding this distinction, you're already ahead of many organizations still trying to apply algorithmic thinking to neural network systems.

The true power of these systems emerges when they're thoughtfully integrated with your organization's unique knowledge, workflows, and objectives. As we continue building our AI nervous system framework, we'll explore how to achieve this integration in ways that amplify human capabilities rather than replacing them.

Key takeaways

- Large language models represent a fundamental shift from deterministic algorithms to probabilistic pattern-recognition systems.
- The transformer architecture enables these models to understand context and generate human-like text.
- Base models are limited by their training data cut-off dates and lack of specific organizational knowledge.
- Web access expands capabilities but requires careful implementation to ensure reliability.
- Retrieval Augmented Generation (RAG) allows models to leverage your organization's proprietary information.
- Building an effective AI brain requires thoughtful model selection, knowledge architecture, integrations, feedback loops and security measures.
- The goal is to augment human capabilities, not replace human judgement.

Questions for reflection

1. What current processes in your organization rely on algorithmic approaches that might benefit from the pattern-recognition capabilities of large language models?
2. What proprietary information in your organization would be most valuable to make accessible to an AI system through RAG?
3. How might the distinction between algorithms and language models change your approach to implementing AI in your organization?
4. What security and governance considerations would be most important for your organization's AI brain?
5. In what ways might web access to current information change the value proposition of AI for your specific use cases?

2

Training the brain

Note to the reader: this chapter uses Formula One racing as its central analogy – a personal passion of mine. If F1 isn't your thing, feel free to substitute any complex system that resonates with you. Perhaps jet engines, the precision of a Michelin-starred kitchen, or even the challenge of identifying which child is calling you in a roomful of pre-schoolers. The principles remain the same regardless of your preferred example, but I'll be sticking with F1 throughout.

Let's start with this. It's not about having more data – it's about teaching your AI brain what deserves attention.

A Formula One car hurtling around the Monaco Grand Prix circuit at 180mph is one of the most data-rich environments on Earth. Over 25,000 sensors monitor everything from tyre pressure and brake temperature to aerodynamic efficiency and fuel consumption. Every millisecond, these sensors generate thousands of data points – engine performance, suspension behaviour, driver biometrics, weather conditions and track surface temperature.

The car produces so much data that if you tried to store it all, you'd fill multiple terabytes during a single race weekend. Yet here's the paradox: despite having access to this overwhelming torrent of information, the difference between winning and losing often comes down to the team's ability to filter signal from noise – to train their collective intelligence on the critical data points that actually matter for performance while ignoring the rest.

The pit crew doesn't need to know the exact temperature of bolt no.3,247 on the rear wing. They need to know that tyre degradation is accelerating in Turn 15, that the driver is experiencing understeer in the chicane, and that fuel consumption suggests a strategic opportunity in lap 23. The art isn't in collecting more data – it's in training your intelligence (human and artificial) to know what deserves attention.

This is exactly what we're doing when we build the data foundation for our organizational AI brain. We're not just feeding it information – we're training it to think like your organization, to pay attention to what matters, and to understand the context that makes information meaningful rather than just accurate.

In the previous chapter we explored how AI brains work fundamentally differently from traditional algorithms – they're pattern recognition systems that learn from examples rather than following predetermined rules. Now we need to train that brain with the right examples from our organization so it can think intelligently about our specific challenges and opportunities.

This chapter is about the organizational principles that determine whether our AI brain becomes genuinely intelligent about our business or just becomes a very expensive way to process irrelevant information.

The protocol principle: why most organizational intelligence is invisible

Before we can train an AI brain effectively, we need to confront an uncomfortable truth about organizational intelligence: most of the knowledge that drives your success doesn't exist in any document, database or system that an AI can access. It lives in conversations, meetings, hallway discussions and the accumulated wisdom that your teams carry in their heads.

This insight comes from Jim Collins' research in *Good to Great*,[1] where he identified what he called the 'protocol principle'. Collins found that companies that sustained exceptional performance over time had one crucial characteristic – they invested extraordinary effort in mapping and organizing how they communicated with one another. The breakthrough teams weren't just good at their work – they were exceptionally good at articulating how they did their work, why they made specific decisions, and what knowledge patterns led to success.

Collins discovered that average companies treated communication as an informal, unstructured process. People knew things, but that knowledge remained locked in individual heads or buried in casual conversations. Great companies, by contrast, developed sophisticated protocols for capturing, organizing and sharing the intelligence that actually drove their performance.

This finding has profound implications for building AI brains. You cannot train an artificial intelligence to think like your organization if your organization's actual thinking processes are invisible, undocumented or trapped in formats that AI systems cannot access.

The hidden intelligence problem

Consider what happens in your organization when someone needs to make a critical decision. They might:

- Have a quick conversation with a colleague who faced a similar situation last year.
- Reference an unwritten rule that 'everyone knows' but isn't documented anywhere.
- Apply lessons learned from a project that was never formally captured.

[1]Collins, J. (2001) *Good to Great: Why Some Companies Make the Leap… and Others Don't*. London: Random House Business.

- Use institutional knowledge that exists only in someone's memory from a meeting three months ago.
- Combine insights from multiple informal sources in ways that would be impossible to replicate.

This is your organization's actual intelligence in action – but none of it is accessible to an AI brain trying to learn how your organization thinks.

The communication debt crisis

Most organizations have accumulated massive 'communication debt' – the gap between what they know and what they've actually articulated in ways that can be shared, referenced and learned from. This debt manifests in several ways:

- **Process knowledge**. Teams know how to do complex work, but the actual steps, decision points, and quality standards exist only in their heads.
- **Contextual wisdom**. People understand why certain approaches work in their specific environment, but this context never gets captured.
- **Relationship intelligence**. Critical knowledge about customers', partners' and stakeholders' lives in informal relationships rather than accessible systems.
- **Problem-solving patterns**. Teams have developed sophisticated approaches to recurring challenges, but these patterns remain invisible to anyone who wasn't involved.

The protocol principle suggests that before you can build an effective AI brain, you need to do the hard work of making your organizational intelligence visible and structured.

From invisible to trainable intelligence

The most successful AI implementations begin not with technology selection, but with what Collins would recognize as protocol development – systematic efforts to capture and organize the intelligence that actually drives organizational performance. This means establishing new communication protocols that transform invisible knowledge into trainable intelligence:

- **Decision documentation**. Moving from 'We decided X' to 'We decided X because of factors Y and Z, considering alternatives A and B'.
- **Process articulation**. Transforming tribal knowledge into explicit procedures that capture not just what to do, but why and when to do it.
- **Context capture**. Recording not just outcomes, but the reasoning, constraints, and environmental factors that influenced decisions.
- **Pattern recognition**. Identifying and documenting the recurring approaches that lead to success in your specific context.

The F1 analogy becomes even more relevant here. Racing teams that consistently win championships don't just collect sensor data – they've developed sophisticated protocols for capturing the reasoning behind strategic decisions, the contextual factors that influence performance, and the patterns that separate good race craft from great race craft. They've made their collective intelligence visible and learnable.

This is the foundational work that must happen before any AI brain training can be effective. You cannot teach an AI to think like your organization if your organization's thinking remains largely invisible to itself.

The big data mistake we all made

Throughout much of the 2010s, the business world became obsessed with collecting everything, just like early racing teams that tried to monitor every possible component of their cars simultaneously – the 'big data' era. Conferences abounded on big data and there were big data experts flooding Twitter (back when it was) with their strategies. Sound familiar?

'Data is the new oil', declared Clive Humby, creator of Tesco's Clubcard,[2] in a phrase that became the rallying cry for an entire industry. The analogy was seductive – just as oil had powered the Industrial Revolution, data would fuel digital transformation. Companies rushed to drill for data wherever they could find it, convinced that somewhere in the vast lakes of information they were accumulating lay the insights that would revolutionize their businesses.

The infrastructure certainly supported this optimism. As Silicon Valley veteran Tim O'Reilly observed at the time, 'There is more data than I thought would ever be possible'.[3] The data universe was expanding exponentially – mobile phones were generating location data, social networks were capturing behaviour patterns, and sensors were proliferating across every industry. 'All these data subsystems are starting to coalesce into this operating system that we all work with', O'Reilly noted, watching companies build entire business models around data collection and analysis.

The mantra was simple – more sensors, more data, more insights. Organizations installed tracking systems everywhere they could. They monitored website visits down to millisecond-level mouse movements. They stored every email, every document, every piece of digital exhaust their operations produced. The assumption was that more data automatically meant

---

[2]www.theguardian.com/technology/2013/aug/23/tech-giants-data

[3]O'Reilly, T. (2013) 'Open data and algorithmic regulation', O'Reilly Radar. www.oreilly.com/radar/open-data-and-algorithmic-regulation/

better decisions – like believing that more sensors automatically make a faster race car.

We learned the hard way that this wasn't true. Just as F1 teams discovered that processing 25,000 sensors simultaneously can overwhelm decision-making rather than improve it, organizations found that drowning their analysts and AI systems in raw data often made them less intelligent, not more. The signal got lost in the noise. Decision-makers were paralysed by information overload. AI models trained on massive, unfocused datasets often performed worse than those trained on smaller, carefully curated ones.

The breakthrough came when organizations started asking a different question. Instead of 'How can we collect more data?' they began asking, 'What information do our teams actually pay attention to, and why?'

The most successful F1 teams now use sophisticated filtering systems that surface the 50–100 critical data points that actually influence race strategy, while using the other 24,950 sensors primarily for background monitoring and historical analysis. They've learned that intelligence isn't about processing everything – it's about knowing what deserves immediate attention versus what provides valuable context over time.

What your teams really pay attention to

Before you design any AI system, you need to understand how knowledge currently flows through your organization. This requires honest conversations with your teams about where they actually go to get information when they need to make decisions. The reality is usually quite different from what the org chart suggests.

Your teams probably don't spend much time digging through the archive of documents stored on shared drives. They don't regularly consult the comprehensive policy manuals gathering digital dust in your knowledge management system. Instead, they pay attention to the information that regularly rises to the top:

- The dashboard they check every morning that shows key performance indicators.
- The most recent case studies that demonstrate what worked (or didn't work) in similar situations.
- The up-to-date patient records, customer profiles, or project status reports that reflect current reality.
- The informal channels where institutional knowledge gets shared – slack conversations, team meetings and quick hallway consultations.

This isn't laziness or poor information hygiene, it's intelligent prioritization. Your teams have learned, through experience, which information sources provide the highest signal-to-noise ratio for their daily work. They've developed sophisticated filtering mechanisms that help them focus on what matters most.

But here's where AI can transform the equation – while humans excel at identifying what's immediately relevant, we're terrible at processing long-term patterns across massive datasets. We can't hold ten years of customer interactions in our heads simultaneously. We can't spot subtle correlations across thousands of variables. We can't remember every edge case that happened five years ago that might be relevant to today's decision. This is where AI systems excel – not in replacing human judgement about what's immediately important, but in surfacing long-term patterns and historical context that human cognition simply can't process effectively.

The art of intelligent attention

The most successful AI implementations blend human intelligence about what's immediately relevant with AI's ability to process vast historical context.

Think of it as combining the F1 pit crew's real-time expertise with a computer's ability to analyse every lap time, tyre temperature and fuel consumption pattern from the last decade of racing. This requires a fundamental shift in how you think about data preparation for AI. Instead of trying to feed your AI everything you have, you need to develop organizational expertise in three critical areas:

1. **The knowledge cut-off problem**. Pre-trained AI models are snapshots in time, like an F1 car that only has data from last season's races. Even the most current models have knowledge cut-offs that create dangerous gaps in rapidly evolving fields. GPT-4o claims an October 2023 cut-off but shows inconsistent knowledge of events even from April 2023. For businesses operating in dynamic environments, this isn't just inconvenient – it's potentially catastrophic.
2. **The domain expertise gap**. Generic AI models lack deep knowledge in specialized fields, like trying to run an F1 race with sensors calibrated for a family sedan.[4] The models simply lacked the nuanced, domain-specific knowledge required for reliable professional application.
3. **The organizational context blind spot**. Most critically for business applications, generic AI models know nothing about your organization's unique data patterns and decision-making context. They can't access your internal policies, understand your unique processes, or draw on your institutional knowledge. They're operating blind to the very context that makes their advice valuable – like an F1 strategist trying to make pit stop decisions without knowing which car they're working with.

---

[4]Ruberg, S., Menon, S. and Demanuele, C. (2023) 'Resolving the Credibility Crisis: Recommendations for Improving Predictive Algorithms for Clinical Utility', *Harvard Data Science Review*, 5(4). doi: 10.1162/99608f92.c1292c54.

The difference isn't in the underlying technology – it's in how well you've trained your AI brain to understand and think about your specific organizational context.

Solving the oracle problem: capturing irreplaceable institutional memory

Every organization has them – the people who seem to know everything. They're the ones everyone turns to when the system breaks down, when a client has an unusual request, or when someone needs to understand 'how we have always done things'. They might be the receptionist who's been at the front desk for twenty years, the operations manager who worked with the founding team, or the senior engineer who remembers why certain decisions were made a decade ago.

These organizational oracles are invaluable. They carry institutional memory that spans generations of employees, understand the subtle contexts that shape how your organization really works, and can navigate complex situations that would stump someone reading from a manual. They know not just what the policies say, but why those policies exist and when it makes sense to bend them. But they also represent your organization's greatest knowledge risk.

The oracle dependency crisis

The oracle problem manifests when organizations become overly dependent on the institutional knowledge stored in one or two key individuals. These people become single points of failure for critical organizational intelligence:

- **Historical context** – They know why certain decisions were made, what was tried before, and what the consequences were.

- **Relationship intelligence** – they understand the personalities, preferences and histories of key clients, partners and stakeholders.
- **Process nuance** – they know when to follow procedures exactly and when situational judgement should override standard practice.
- **Cultural knowledge** – they understand the unwritten rules, communication patterns, and values that actually drive organizational behaviour.
- **Crisis memory** – they remember how the organization navigated previous challenges, what worked and what didn't.

The problem becomes acute when these oracles approach retirement, change roles, or – heaven forbid – walk out the door unexpectedly. Suddenly, large chunks of organizational intelligence disappear overnight. Projects stall because no one remembers why certain approaches were chosen. Client relationships suffer because their history and preferences exist only in someone's memory. Problem-solving becomes harder because institutional learning has literally walked out the building.

Why traditional knowledge management fails oracles

Most organizations try to solve the oracle problem through traditional documentation approaches – asking these key individuals to write down what they know. This rarely works effectively for several reasons:

- **Tacit knowledge**. Much oracle knowledge is experiential and contextual, difficult to capture in written procedures.
- **Time constraints**. Oracles are usually too busy being consulted on current issues to systematically document their knowledge.
- **Knowledge interconnectedness**. Oracle knowledge is deeply interconnected – extracting one piece often requires explaining five others.

- **Timing mismatch**. By the time organizations realize they need to capture oracle knowledge, it's often too late to do it systematically.

AI brains as oracle insurance

Training an AI brain provides a sophisticated solution to the oracle problem. Unlike traditional documentation, AI systems can capture and organize the complex, interconnected knowledge that oracles carry. Here's how.

- **Conversational knowledge capture**. Instead of asking oracles to write formal documentation, you can have them engage in recorded conversations with AI systems about different scenarios, decisions and challenges. The AI brain learns from these natural explanations and can later reference them when similar situations arise.
- **Pattern recognition across time**. AI brains can identify patterns in oracle decision-making that even the oracles themselves might not consciously recognize. By analysing years of their recommendations and explanations, AI systems can learn the underlying principles that guide their judgement.
- **Contextual memory storage**. AI brains can store not just facts, but the rich context around why certain decisions were made, what alternatives were considered, and what environmental factors influenced outcomes.
- **Scenario-based learning**. You can systematically walk through different scenarios with your oracles, recording their thinking process and decision frameworks. The AI brain learns from these examples and can apply similar reasoning to new situations.
- **Cross-reference capability**. Unlike human memory, AI brains can instantly cross-reference oracle knowledge with current data, policies, and changing circumstances, providing recommendations that blend institutional wisdom with current realities.

The oracle transition strategy

The most effective approach to solving the oracle problem involves partnering your organizational oracles with AI brain development:

- **Systematic knowledge mapping**. Work with oracles to identify the key areas where their knowledge is most critical and irreplaceable.
- **Conversational documentation**. Record regular sessions where oracles explain their reasoning about different types of decisions.
- **Scenario planning**. Walk through various 'what if' situations and capture how oracles would approach each challenge.
- **Decision pattern analysis**. Have AI systems analyse the oracle's historical recommendations to identify underlying principles.
- **Continuous learning**. Build processes where the AI brain continues learning from oracle interactions over time.

Beyond individual oracles: collective intelligence

The ultimate goal isn't just to replicate individual oracle knowledge, but to create AI brains that combine the wisdom of multiple organizational oracles over time. Your AI brain can become a repository of collective institutional intelligence that grows stronger with each oracle's contribution and continues learning long after any individual has moved on.

This transforms the oracle problem from a risk into an opportunity. Instead of worrying about knowledge walking out the door, you're building systems that capture, organize and make accessible the collective wisdom of everyone who contributes to your organization's intelligence over time.

Think of your AI brain as creating an immortal oracle – one that never retires, never gets sick, and never takes their knowledge to a competitor. This oracle doesn't replace human judgement and relationship skills, but it ensures that the hard-won institutional wisdom that makes your organization unique is preserved, accessible and continuously enhanced for future generations. Because the goal isn't to eliminate the need for experienced people – it's to ensure that their wisdom outlasts their tenure and continues benefiting your organization long after they've moved on to their next adventure.

The four training principles for organizational AI brains

Building an effective AI brain requires four foundational training principles that organizations must establish before selecting any tools or technologies. Think of these as the equivalent of an F1 team's driver development program – the systematic approach that transforms raw capability into championship-level intelligence.

Training principle 1: Cognitive mapping

Before you can train your AI brain effectively, you need to map how intelligence currently flows through your organization. This isn't about cataloguing every document you have – it's about understanding the cognitive patterns that drive real decisions.

Start by asking your teams the fundamental question: 'When you need to make a decision or solve a problem, where does your brain actually go to get information?' The answers will often surprise you and reveal the true intelligence architecture of your organization.

The most effective AI implementations understand that organizational knowledge exists in layers, just like F1 teams organize their race data. Before we dive into the specific tiers, it's important to understand that these aren't just about organizing documents – they represent how human attention and AI processing can work together to create superior intelligence.

McKinsey's research on successful enterprise AI reveals that organizations should structure their knowledge into four cognitive tiers, based on how frequently the information is accessed and its impact on decision-making:

- **Tier 1: Active cognitive load** – information teams use daily for immediate decisions.
- **Tier 2: Reference cognitive load** – knowledge accessed periodically for context and guidance.
- **Tier 3: Background cognitive load** – long-term patterns that inform strategic thinking.
- **Tier 4: Archived cognitive load** – historical knowledge accessed rarely but valuable for precedent.

Each tier requires different approaches to AI integration, with the goal being to augment human cognitive strengths while compensating for our limitations. Let's examine each tier in detail.

Tier 1: Active cognitive load

This tier represents the information your teams process daily – CRM dashboards, real-time metrics and current project status reports. It's your highest-signal data because teams have validated its importance through repeated use.

Human strengths

- Excellent at quickly identifying what's immediately relevant.
- Strong contextual understanding of why this data matters now.
- Intuitive grasp of how current metrics relate to immediate decisions.

AI strengths

- Can monitor and process all active data streams simultaneously.
- No attention fatigue when monitoring real-time dashboards.
- Can instantly recall and connect current data to historical patterns.

Tier 2: Reference cognitive load

This encompasses knowledge accessed for deeper context – recent case studies, updated procedures and current best practices. This information provides crucial cognitive scaffolding when needed.

Human strengths

- Excellent at determining when reference information is needed.
- Good at contextualizing best practices to specific situations.
- Strong ability to adapt procedures based on current circumstances.

AI strengths

- Can instantly access and process the entire reference knowledge base.
- No memory limitations when recalling procedures or best practices.
- Can systematically compare current situations to reference cases.

Tier 3: Background cognitive load

This tier contains long-term patterns that individual humans struggle to process – years of customer interactions, operational trends and historical project outcomes. This is where AI can dramatically augment human cognition.

Human strengths

- Good at identifying which long-term patterns might be relevant.
- Strong intuitive sense for outliers or anomalies in patterns.
- Excellent at contextualizing why historical patterns matter.

AI strengths

- Can process years of data to identify subtle patterns humans miss.
- No cognitive limitations when analysing complex historical trends.
- Can detect correlations across massive datasets spanning long time periods.

Tier 4: Archived cognitive load

This tier contains vast collections of historical knowledge that may contain valuable insights but require sophisticated filtering to avoid cognitive overload. This should be accessed selectively for historical context when specific patterns become relevant.

Human strengths

- Good at determining when archived information might be valuable.
- Strong ability to judge the relevance of historical precedents.
- Excellent at interpreting historical context through modern lenses.

AI strengths

- Can search and process entire archives instantly.
- No retrieval limitations when accessing historical information.
- Can systematically connect archived knowledge to current situations.
- Can identify relevant historical edge cases from massive archives.

The ideal approach combines human strengths in determining relevance and context with AI's capabilities for comprehensive processing, pattern recognition, and recall across all four tiers – creating an intelligence system greater than either could achieve alone.

The key insight is that most organizations get this backwards, like F1 teams that focus on monitoring every bolt temperature while ignoring the critical real-time data that determines race strategy. Your AI brain needs to learn the same cognitive prioritization that your experienced teams have developed through practice.

Training principle 2: Intelligence quality standards

Training an effective AI brain requires the same attention to quality that F1 teams apply to their data streams. Poor quality information doesn't just reduce your AI brain's performance – it can actively teach it to think incorrectly about your organization.

Just as F1 teams calibrate their sensors to specific accuracy standards, organizations need to establish quality benchmarks for their own organizations; standards you can review and measure over time; and dimensional standards that measure different aspects of your implementation:

- **Accuracy**: information correctness that reflects real-world.
- **Completeness**: cognitive coverage without missing critical context.
- **Consistency**: uniform thinking patterns across information sources.
- **Timeliness**: current relevance for active decision-making.
- **Uniqueness**: elimination of conflicting or duplicate information.
- **Validity**: adherence to organizational reasoning patterns and standards.

Every organization will take a slightly different approach to this but the central point here is that we need to have clear benchmarks and standards for our own organizations. Taking the work that someone has generically done somewhere else and trying to apply it to your own AI brain is like trying to transplant information from somebody else's head.

Much like Neo in *The Matrix*, you can download information straight onto your own way of working. But it's going to take some real time in the cognitive dojo to improve your skill set for it to fully assimilate into the organization.

But quality isn't just about technical accuracy. It's also about cognitive governance – establishing clear ownership of different types of organizational intelligence, update processes that maintain freshness, and validation workflows that ensure your AI brain learns to think correctly about your business context. Think of this as establishing the equivalent of an F1 team's data protocols. The brain can only be as intelligent as the examples it learns from.

Training principle 3: Cognitive change management

Here's where most AI implementations fail – they treat building organizational intelligence as a purely technical challenge rather than an organizational transformation. Research shows that 75 per cent[5] of companies struggle with AI adoption due to organizational factors, not technical limitations.

Training an effective AI brain requires a 2:1 investment ratio – two dollars in cognitive change management for every dollar in technical build. This isn't about training people to use new tools – it's about fundamentally expanding how intelligence operates within your organization.

Consider Airbnb's approach with its 'Data University' – it didn't just deploy AI tools, it built an organizational culture that could effectively leverage and contribute to AI intelligence. It created customized programs with role-specific AI literacy, hands-on experience with low-risk pilot programs, and cross-functional communities that could enhance the AI brain's learning over time.[6]

---

[5]www.bcg.com/press/24october2024-ai-adoption-in-2024-74-of-companies-struggle-to-achieve-and-scale-value

[6]Christian, B. (2017) 'To increase data skills, Airbnb has started its own university', *Wired*, 7 December. Available at: www.wired.com/story/airbnb-in-house-data-university-employee-skills/ (accessed 8 December 2025).

Your AI change strategy should address three key areas:

- **Leadership alignment.** C-suite understanding of how AI brains learn and develop, with clear intelligence strategy communication and investment allocation tied to cognitive development objectives.
- **Employee partnership.** Role-specific training that helps team members understand how to effectively collaborate with and train the AI brain, hands-on pilot programmes that demonstrate augmented intelligence in action, and clear career development paths that show how AI enhances rather than threatens human cognitive contribution.
- **Resistance to change.** Transparent communication about how AI brains learn and develop organizational intelligence, gradual implementation that allows teams to experience cognitive augmentation benefits first-hand, and comprehensive support systems that help people adapt to working with artificial intelligence.

Remember: you're not just implementing technology – you're expanding your organization's collective intelligence. The AI brain learns from how your organization thinks, communicates and makes decisions. If your people don't understand and actively contribute to this process, your AI brain will never develop sophisticated organizational intelligence.

Training principle 4: Neural integration architecture

The fourth training principle focuses on how your AI brain integrates with your organization's existing systems and workflows. This isn't just about technical integration – it's about designing knowledge pathways that allow artificial and human intelligence to work together seamlessly – just like the ones in your own head.

Your AI brain needs sophisticated connections to existing cognitive systems – core business intelligence (CRMs, ERPs, knowledge bases), communication networks (email, chat, collaboration tools), authentication and access patterns that match human cognitive permissions, and workflow integration that allows AI insights to influence real decision-making processes.

But more importantly, you need to design feedback loops that allow your AI brain to continuously learn from how it's actually being used within your organization. This includes feedback collection that teaches the AI brain when its reasoning is helpful versus when it misses the mark, performance monitoring that tracks not just accuracy but cognitive usefulness in real business contexts, and continuous learning processes that help the AI brain adapt as your organization's thinking evolves.

Think of this as building the neural pathways that connect your AI brain to your organization's collective intelligence. Just like our F1 teams have sophisticated communication systems that allow real-time data to influence split-second strategic decisions, your AI brain needs routes that allow it to participate meaningfully in your organization's processes.

Teaching your AI brain organizational intelligence

Only after establishing these four training principles should you begin selecting specific AI tools and technologies. The tools should serve your AI development strategy, not dictate it.

For most organizations, Retrieval Augmented Generation (RAG) emerges as the optimal training approach for AI brains. Think of RAG as giving your AI brain a research team that can instantly access your organization's collective memory while maintaining the conversational and reasoning capabilities of advanced AI models.

When you ask your AI brain a question, RAG systems first search your organizational knowledge base for relevant context, then provide that information to the AI model along with your question. The result is responses that demonstrate genuine organizational intelligence – thinking that's grounded in your actual experience, policies and decision-making frameworks while maintaining the sophisticated reasoning capabilities that make AI valuable.

The beauty of RAG for training AI brains is that it addresses the three fundamental limitations we discussed earlier:

1. **Knowledge currency**: you can continuously update your AI brain's knowledge without retraining the underlying model.
2. **Domain intelligence**: you can teach your AI brain your organization's specialized knowledge and reasoning patterns.
3. **Organizational context**: the AI brain develops genuine understanding of your specific cognitive context and decision-making frameworks.

RAG allows your AI brain to develop increasingly sophisticated understanding of your organization over time, learning from each interaction and continuously expanding its cognitive capabilities.

Having a well-trained AI brain is only valuable if you know how to deploy it strategically. The next challenge is determining which specific business problems your AI brain should tackle first, and how to give it clear, actionable instructions that translate your organizational intelligence into measurable results.

The intelligence development paradox

Here's the paradox most organizations face – the technical implementation of AI brains has never been easier, but developing genuine organizational intelligence has never been more complex. Cloud platforms provide RAG capabilities out-of-the-box, embedding models are becoming commoditized, and vector databases are increasingly accessible. But successfully training an AI brain to think intelligently about your organization requires solving challenges that have nothing to do with technology:

- How do you maintain quality across diverse information sources and communication patterns?
- How do you ensure organizational intelligence stays current as your business thinking evolves?
- How do you balance accessibility with security and privacy concerns?
- How do you measure and improve AI brain intelligence in real business contexts?
- How do you build capabilities that survive personnel changes and organizational evolution?

These are organizational intelligence challenges, not technical ones. The organizations that solve them well position themselves to benefit from every new AI capability that emerges. Those that don't will find themselves constantly upgrading to the latest AI technology without ever achieving sustainable organizational intelligence.

Training for cognitive evolution

The goal isn't to train today's AI brain perfectly – it's to build organizational capabilities for continuous cognitive development that can evolve with rapidly advancing AI capabilities. This means creating cognitive systems that are going to get MASS (Modular, Adaptive, Scalable and Sustainable) adoption. What's MASS, I hear you cry?

- **Modular.** Your intelligence training processes should work with different AI models and vendors as capabilities evolve, like how F1 teams develop driver skills that transfer across different car designs.
- **Adaptive.** Your cognitive architecture should be able to incorporate new AI capabilities as they emerge without disrupting core organizational intelligence.
- **Scalable.** Your approach should grow with your organization's cognitive maturity without requiring complete retraining, allowing your AI brain to become more sophisticated over time.
- **Sustainable.** Your organizational intelligence development processes should persist beyond any specific technology or vendor, building lasting cognitive capabilities.

The path forward: from training to strategic deployment

Organizations with robust cognitive development foundations will be best positioned to capitalize on emerging AI opportunities while avoiding the 80 per cent failure rate that plagues generic AI implementations. But success requires fundamentally changing how we think about AI brain development.

The big data era taught us that more information isn't automatically better intelligence. The F1 teams that win championships aren't the ones with the most sensors – they're the ones with the best expertise in developing intelligence from those sensors. Similarly, the organizations that will thrive with AI aren't those with the most data, but those with the best organizational capabilities for training artificial intelligence to think meaningfully about their specific challenges and opportunities.

But training your AI brain is only the beginning. The protocol principle shows us that great organizations excel not just at developing intelligence, but at deploying that intelligence strategically across their operations. They know how to identify the specific situations where their organizational intelligence can create the most value, and they have systematic approaches for putting that intelligence to work.

This means treating AI brain implementation as both a cognitive development challenge and a strategic deployment challenge. You need equal investment in training capabilities and the organizational frameworks that determine how and where your AI brain gets applied to real business problems.

The next chapter will show you how to make that strategic leap from a well-trained AI brain to systematic organizational value creation. We'll explore how to identify the specific use cases where your trained AI brain can deliver the greatest impact, how to prioritize AI initiatives based on effort versus return, and how to translate your organizational intelligence into clear, actionable instructions that drive measurable business results. The chapter is about answering the critical question: 'Now that we have a smart AI brain that understands our organization, what specific problems should we ask it to solve, and how do we ensure it applies our intelligence in ways that create real value?'

Developing organizational intelligence is meaningless unless you can deploy it strategically. The most beautifully trained AI brain in the world won't help your organization if you can't figure out what to ask it to do – or if you ask it to work on the wrong problems.

The brain is just the beginning. Next, we need to learn how to put that intelligence to work in the service of your mission and objectives.

Key takeaways

- Intelligence isn't about more data, it's about trained attention to what deserves focus.

- Make invisible knowledge visible – protocols turn tribal wisdom into trainable context.
- Quality standards are cognitive guardrails, not paperwork.
- RAG is the pragmatic path for organizational intelligence – current, contextual and cost-effective.
- Build feedback loops and ownership so the brain keeps learning as the business changes.

Questions for reflection

1. What do your teams actually pay attention to daily, and how is that captured today?
2. Which single quality dimension – accuracy, completeness, consistency, timeliness, uniqueness, validity – most needs work?
3. Where would a RAG approach immediately improve answers your teams seek weekly?
4. Who is responsible for keeping organizational intelligence fresh across functions?
5. What failure mode have you seen already that better protocols would have prevented?

3

Instructing your AI brain

Why we tolerate inefficiency at work

In his provocative book *Bullshit Jobs*, anthropologist David Graeber[1] argues that a significant proportion of modern work – perhaps as much as 40 per cent – consists of tasks that even the workers themselves consider pointless or meaningless. These aren't just trivial activities, they're entire roles and processes that have emerged to serve organizational theatre rather than organizational purpose.

Graeber identified several categories of what he termed 'bullshit jobs' – flunkies who exist primarily to make their superiors feel important, goons whose roles involve aggression or deception, duct tapers who temporarily fix problems that should be solved permanently, box tickers who exist to create the appearance of something being done, and taskmasters who assign work to others without adding value themselves.

The economic cost of this inefficiency is staggering. Research from Atlassian found that the average employee attends sixty-two meetings per month,[2] half of which are considered time wasted. McKinsey's research suggests that

---

[1]Graeber, D. (2018) *Bullshit Jobs: A Theory*. London: Penguin.
[2]www.atlassian.com/blog/workplace-woes-meetings

employees spend 20 per cent of their weeks searching for and gathering information.[3]

A 2023 study by Asana[4] revealed that knowledge workers spend only 27 per cent of their day on the skilled work they were actually hired to do. The remaining time is consumed by coordinating work (60 per cent) and what they termed 'work about work' – the tasks that surround the actual work, like searching for documents, chasing approvals, switching between apps and managing shifting priorities.

Research suggests that unproductive or poorly run meetings cost US organizations somewhere between $37 billion and nearly $399 billion every year. That's not a rounding error – it's a structural leak in how modern work happens. And yet, we tolerate it. We accept calendar invitations without agendas or outcomes. We prepare reports no one reads, we sit through recurring meetings out of habit rather than necessity, and we navigate approval chains that grow in length but not in value. Over time, this isn't just inefficiency – it's cultural acceptance. We've normalized collaboration theatre, where participation is mistaken for progress, and where time becomes the silent casualty.[5] Why? Because confronting inefficiency requires confronting people, and their identities, their job security, their sense of purpose. It's easier to tolerate the slow degradation of productivity than to have the difficult conversation about whether someone's entire role needs to exist.

This is the context into which AI arrives, not as a solution looking for a problem but as a catalyst that forces us to ask the questions we have been avoiding:

- What work actually matters?
- What are we doing simply because we have always done it?

---

[3]www.mckinsey.com/industries/technology-media-and-telecommunications/our-insights/the-social-economy

[4]https://asana.com/resources/anatomy-of-work

[5]www.businessinsider.com/37-billion-is-lost-every-year-on-these-meeting-mistakes-2014-4

- What could we eliminate entirely if we had the courage to admit it never added value in the first place?

The steep hill paradox

I sit in my seat, seatbelt fastened, watching the cabin crew move through their final checks. Then I hear it, the distinctive 'ping ping' that signals we have been cleared for take-off. Only then do I reach up and activate the noise-cancelling on my headphones. It's become a ritual – that auditory cocoon right before the plane begins its rush down the runway.

What follows is a paradox I have never quite got used to. As the aircraft races down the runway, pilots deploy the flaps to generate lift. At this critical moment, right when the plane leaves the ground, passengers often experience that unsettling sensation of momentary descent, as if the aircraft might drop back to earth. In reality, this is precisely when the plane is accelerating most dramatically, converting speed into altitude.

This experience perfectly illustrates our psychological resistance to change. The moment when we commit to a new path feels most perilous. We perceive danger and loss of control, yet it is exactly when we are gaining the momentum needed for transformation. Just as passengers grip their armrests during take-off, organizations cling to familiar processes during change initiatives, even when those processes are clearly inefficient. The inverse is often also true. Consider the static bike rider in the spin class. They can tolerate that slow slog up the hill for the last ten minutes just fine because it rises in incremental steps.

Picture Sarah, our determined spin enthusiast, pedalling away while the instructor cheerfully announces 'Just one more level!' (five times in a row). Her legs burn, sweat cascades down her face, and yet she continues turning that resistance knob when prompted. Why? Because each tiny increment feels manageable, even as the cumulative effect is transforming her quads into quivering jelly. The same Sarah who would vigorously protest if asked to jump immediately to maximum resistance will happily endure the torture of gradual intensification, all while paying $35 for the privilege!

Renewal is often like this. We tolerate slow degradation of quality over time, accepting inefficiencies that compound gradually. But then it takes a significant jolt to the system for us to adopt new technology. This pattern repeats across industries and contexts:

- **Adoption of messaging platforms in companies.** For years, organizations relied on email despite its inefficiencies, lost threads, unclear action items, and information silos. Yet companies continued using it because 'that's how we have always communicated'. It took the rise of Slack and Microsoft Teams, combined with the pressure of remote work, to break this pattern. The pandemic provided the jolt that made synchronous, threaded communication not just preferable but necessary.
- **Online church pre-Covid.** Religious institutions had the technology to stream services online for over a decade, yet most resisted. The objections were always the same: 'People need to be physically present', 'It's not the same experience', 'We will lose our sense of community'. Then Covid-19 forced churches to go digital overnight. What was once considered impossible became standard practice within weeks. Interestingly, many congregations discovered they could reach homebound members, young families with small children, and geographically distant communities in ways they never had before. The crisis revealed that the resistance was never really about capability, it was about challenging the status quo.
- **BYOD, the BlackBerry to iPhone moment.** Corporate IT departments built entire infrastructure around BlackBerry devices. They cited security, manageability, and enterprise integration as

> reasons why consumer devices like the iPhone could never work in business environments. Then employees started bringing their iPhones to work anyway. The consumerization of IT was not driven by IT departments – it was driven by users who experienced superior technology in their personal lives and refused to accept inferior tools at work. Organizations eventually had to adapt their policies to accommodate the devices people actually wanted to use.

These examples reveal a crucial insight – change requires new incentives, and they have to be big enough to overcome the inertia of the old way of doing things. The incentive cannot be marginal improvement. It needs to be transformative enough to justify the disruption, retraining and psychological adjustment that change demands.

Charlie Munger, Warren Buffett's long-time business partner, famously said: 'Show me the incentive and I'll show you the outcome.' If you want to understand why any system behaves the way it does, why people make the decisions they make, why organizations resist change, why inefficiencies persist, you need to understand the incentives. The problem is that most organizational incentives reward stability over innovation, compliance over creativity, and avoiding failure over achieving success.

This is why first we have to design new incentives if we want to catalyse real change. Before introducing AI tools, before redesigning workflows, before training teams on new systems, we need to examine and redesign the underlying incentive structures that govern behaviour. What gets measured gets managed, and what gets rewarded gets repeated. If your organization rewards people for looking busy rather than being productive, for attending meetings rather than making decisions, for process compliance rather than outcome achievement, then no amount of AI implementation will transform how work gets done.

Too often we see something new and shiny like AI and start cooking up solutions, rather than asking ourselves what poor performance of existing systems we have accepted or learned to tolerate over time. The reality is that there are people in your organization who could be doing much more if you actually had the incentive to motivate them, challenge them, or correct them. But that requires confrontation. AI therefore seems a good excuse to challenge this workflow. Many of the big tech companies have arguably used AI as a scapegoat for layoffs, without actually citing the cooling of the economy, global conflict, oil prices, or acknowledging their own bloat and over-ambition.

Designing the right incentives: a lesson from AI

This brings us to a useful framework borrowed from the world of artificial intelligence itself. When AI researchers build systems, they work with two distinct concepts: objective functions and reward functions. Understanding the difference is not just technically interesting – it is essential for anyone trying to design better incentives for humans. The objective function is the 'what'. It defines the end goal. Get the user to click. Reduce costs. Maximize engagement. It is the destination on the map. The reward function is the 'how'. It provides the signals that tell the system it is moving in the right direction. Every click earns a point. Every cost reduction triggers a bonus. These are the breadcrumbs on the trail.

Here is where it gets interesting: most AI disasters happen when these two become misaligned. Consider social media algorithms. The objective function is 'maximize engagement'. The reward function is 'optimize for time on platform'. Technically aligned, yes? Except the system discovered that outrage keeps people scrolling longer than joy. The objective was achieved. The reward was earned. And society became more polarized as a result. The AI did exactly what we asked. We just asked the wrong question.

The parallel to organizational life is striking. Think about that spin class again. Sarah's objective function might be 'get fitter'. But her immediate reward function – the one that keeps her turning that resistance knob – is 'survive the next thirty seconds without falling off the bike'. These are not the same thing. One is about long-term transformation. The other is about immediate endurance. The instructor's genius is in designing reward signals (encouragement, music, the promise of 'just one more minute') that keep Sarah moving towards the objective even when her legs are screaming at her to stop. Now apply this to your organization.

What is the stated objective? Probably something like 'deliver excellent customer service' or 'drive innovation' or 'increase efficiency'. Noble goals. But what are the actual reward signals your people experience day to day? The metrics on their dashboards, the behaviours that get praised in meetings, the actions that lead to promotions?

If your objective is 'innovation' but your reward function is 'do not make mistakes', you have created the organizational equivalent of a social media algorithm optimizing for outrage. The system will do exactly what you have incentivized it to do. It will play it safe. It will avoid risk. It will innovate only in the most marginal, defensible ways. This is why, before any AI initiative, you need to spend time – real time – mapping out your human objective and reward functions. Interview your customers. Shadow your staff. Understand what 'good' actually feels like, not just what it measures like.

I have worked with organizations that deployed sophisticated AI only to discover they had optimized for the wrong thing entirely: sales teams where the AI maximized call volume but tanked close rates; customer service bots that resolved tickets faster while customer satisfaction cratered. The machines did their job perfectly. The humans had not done theirs.

The question is not 'What AI tools should we implement?' The question is, 'What are we actually trying to achieve, and what signals are we currently sending about what matters?' Get that right, and the technology becomes a powerful accelerant. Get it wrong, and you have simply automated your existing dysfunction.

One of the biggest challenges we face when something new arrives with so much hype is to see through the noise to work out what it is actually worth doing with it. To deal with this we can't just stumble into putting AI to work – we have to design for it – and for that we need the right tools. Thankfully, design thinking has given us some of these use cases, and one is user stories.

Designing use cases

The power of the user story – work out what you actually should focus on

What does the user, team member, staffer, supporter, or customer actually want? As a leader, it is highly unlikely, unless you work solo or in a micro business, that you are designing solutions for one person. Therefore, you need to cultivate the skill of empathy, putting yourself in another person's shoes.

What is empathy, and why are we as humans uniquely able to do this? It's worth pausing on this question because empathy isn't just a nice-to-have soft skill – it's actually a sophisticated capability that humans have refined over millennia, and it's fundamental to everything from building products to leading teams to, yes, designing AI systems that actually serve human needs.

Empathy is our ability to step into someone else's shoes and genuinely understand what they're experiencing. Not just intellectually grasp it, but *feel* it in a way that shapes how we respond. And humans are remarkably good at this for several interconnected reasons.

First, we are fundamentally social creatures. We didn't evolve as solitary hunters – we evolved in complex social groups where survival depended on cooperation, communication and understanding what others were thinking and feeling. Your ancestor who could read the room and anticipate how the tribe would react to a proposed hunt had a significant survival advantage over the one who couldn't. This social wiring runs deep – it's why we instinctively mirror each other's facial expressions, why we feel uncomfortable when someone else is embarrassed, why we can watch a film and feel genuine emotion for fictional characters.

Second, we operate in what I think of as 4D – three spatial dimensions plus time. We don't just perceive the present moment – we constantly contextualize everything within a temporal framework. When you're talking to a colleague who seems irritated, you're not just processing their current expression – you're unconsciously drawing on your memory of how they usually behave, what happened in the meeting before this conversation, and perhaps even anticipating how they might feel tomorrow when the pressure has lifted. This temporal depth gives human empathy a richness that's difficult to replicate.

Third, we move through the world dynamically, constantly adapting our understanding based on changing circumstances and social contexts. The empathy you deploy when comforting a grieving friend is different from the empathy you use when negotiating a business deal, which is different again from the empathy you need when teaching a child to ride a bike. We shift between these modes fluidly, often without conscious thought, reading micro-signals and adjusting our approach in real-time. AI just doesn't work this way – it may 'learn' from our conversations with it, but most of the time it doesn't retain all the context of the world you are creating within it.

Fourth, we have this remarkable ability to foresee future scenarios and consequences. We can project ourselves into hypothetical situations that haven't happened yet and imagine how we or others might feel. This is why we can design products for users we haven't met yet, or create policies for situations that don't currently exist.

Finally, we have the ability to learn from past interactions and refine our empathetic understanding over time. Every conversation, every relationship, every observation of human behaviour becomes data that enriches our model of how people work. You learn that your business partner needs time to process big decisions, that your designer colleague responds better to questions than directives, that your CEO values conciseness over blathering on. This accumulated wisdom shapes how you interact with others in increasingly nuanced ways.

Now, here's where it gets interesting. Some of this AI is also able to do, but definitely not all of it. Modern AI systems can process patterns in human behaviour at scale, identify correlations we might miss, and even predict likely responses based on historical data. What they can't do – at least not yet, and perhaps not ever in the same way – is the embodied, lived experience that makes human empathy so contextually rich and adaptable. An AI can tell you that people generally prefer direct communication during crises, but it doesn't *know* what it feels like to receive bad news or to be the person trying to deliver it with compassion. That experiential knowledge shapes human empathy in ways that are difficult to capture in training data. This is where design thinking enters the picture, specifically through a deceptively simple tool – the user story.

If you've worked in product development, you've likely encountered user stories before. They follow a now-familiar template: 'As a [type of user], I want to [action] so that [benefit].' Simple enough, right? But the brilliance isn't in the formula – it's in what the formula forces you to do. A user story makes you stop thinking about solutions and start thinking about people.

Here's why this matters particularly for AI implementation. Most technology projects fail not because the technology doesn't work, but because it solves the wrong problem or solves the right problem in a way that doesn't match how humans actually work. We build elaborate systems that look impressive in demonstrations but gather dust in practice because we started with 'What can we build?' instead of 'What do people actually need?'

User stories force a different starting point. They require empathy – that uniquely human capacity we explored earlier – to become the foundation of your design process. When you write, 'As a customer service representative, I want to access relevant product information while on calls so that I can resolve issues on the first contact', you're not just documenting a requirement. You're stepping into someone else's day, feeling their frustration and understanding their constraints.

The design thinking movement, which originated at Stanford and IDEO and has since spread across organizations globally, recognized something crucial – the people closest to the problem often have the clearest view of what would actually help. But they need structured ways to articulate that knowledge. This is what user stories provide – a framework for translating lived experience into actionable insights.

Think about it: without a user story format, how would that customer service representative describe what they need? They might say 'better systems' or 'more training' or 'faster computers'. These are solutions masquerading as problems. But when you ask them to complete, 'I want to [blank] so that I can [blank]', suddenly you're getting at the underlying need: I want to *access information* so that I can *resolve issues faster*. Now you have something specific to design for, and importantly, something you can test whether you've actually achieved it.

For AI implementation specifically, user stories serve another critical function – they help you identify where AI is actually appropriate. Not everything needs AI. Not everything should be automated. But when you have a clear user story that involves processing large amounts of information quickly, identifying patterns across datasets, or generating variations on content themes, you've likely found a legitimate AI use case.

The exercise of writing user stories also reveals gaps in your understanding. I've run workshops where leaders assumed they knew exactly what their teams needed, only to find that the user stories their teams wrote were completely different from what they'd anticipated. This is valuable discomfort – the kind that prevents you from building expensive solutions to imaginary problems.

What I find particularly powerful about user stories in the AI context is how they combat the 'shiny object syndrome' that plagues so many technology initiatives. When you're dazzled by what AI *can* do – and let's be honest, the capabilities are genuinely impressive – it's easy to start implementing features because they're cool rather than because they're useful. User stories keep you anchored to actual human needs.

There's also something democratic about this approach. When you ask people across your organization to write their own user stories, you're acknowledging that they are the experts in their own work. You're not positioning yourself as the all-knowing leader who will bestow AI solutions from on high. You're creating space for the people who live with these challenges daily to articulate what would genuinely help them.

This ties back to that empathy we discussed earlier – the capacity to understand what someone else experiences. But here's the thing: you can't empathize your way into someone else's job if you've never done it. You can try, and you might get close, but you'll miss the subtle friction points, the workarounds people have developed, the things that look small from the outside but loom large in the daily experience of the work. User stories give those people a voice in the design process. They democratize innovation.

Now, here's where it gets interesting from a practical standpoint. The quality of your user stories directly determines the quality of your AI implementation. A vague user story ('As a manager, I want better reports') will lead to vague solutions. A precise user story ('As a regional sales manager, I want to visualize pipeline progression by stage across my team so that I can identify stalled deals before they jeopardize quarterly targets') gives you something concrete to build towards.

This precision matters enormously when you're working with AI systems because – as we've discussed – these systems respond to clear instructions. The discipline of writing a good user story is remarkably similar to the discipline of writing a good prompt. Both require you to be specific about context, action and desired outcome. Both force you to think through what success actually looks like.

In the exercises that follow throughout this chapter, we'll be using user stories as our primary tool for identifying AI opportunities. Not because it's the only methodology available, but because it consistently produces the most useful results. It keeps us human-centred in a conversation that can easily become technology-centred.

So when I ask you to write user stories for your organization, I'm not asking you to fill out forms. I'm asking you to practice empathy at scale. To step into the shoes of your colleagues, your customers, your stakeholders. To understand not just what they do, but why they do it and what would genuinely make their work more effective, meaningful or enjoyable. Because here's what I've learned – the best AI implementations aren't the ones with the most sophisticated algorithms or the most impressive technical specifications. They're the ones that actually solve real problems for real people. And you can't get there without first understanding what those people actually need. User stories are how we do that understanding at scale.

Why do user stories help us build empathy?

As a [role] I want to [objective] so that I [reward].

This puts us in the role of the user of the tool and combines the objective and reward functions of the user in one statement.

I have found the more concise the user story, the better the user story, usually. But more importantly, perhaps precision is more important than brevity. Prompting AI models to do the work of humans requires precision of language because it is through language that we instruct these models, and it is what they are trained on. Therefore, everything upstream of that prompt, including the user story, is better to be precise than verbose because we are trying in the most specific way we can to articulate the work we do.

I have found in workshop settings that many people find this difficult because, as we touched upon previously, most of us are not that great at actually articulating what we do with our days. It is why timesheets or time tracking in companies can feel limited in their efficacy. You may have spent two hours on that project, but it does not capture what those two hours contained, or if they were of any quality. As such, it is hard to estimate how long things take when we rely upon the lagging indicators of previous time spent. Let alone the issue of estimating how long it will take to do something you have not yet done. This is before we consider the time gap between estimating the thing and doing the thing, which may be disrupted by a technology (sound familiar?) that means you can do that thing faster.

It is for these reasons that I also suggest not writing user stories that are predominantly based on how long something takes, but to be more scrupulous in asking *how* something can be done differently to be *better*; not faster. Or, if cost is a driver, then we may focus on *cheaper* too. The most effective route we have found so far is to have users themselves write their stories. They know their work better than you can assume to do, unless you have done that job before, and even if you have done it before, as we can see now, our context and tools are changing all the time.

Example user stories

Marketing Team:

- As a marketing manager, I want to automate the creation of social media content variations so that I can test different messaging without increasing design team workload.
- As a content strategist, I want to analyse engagement metrics across platforms in a single dashboard so that I can quickly identify which content themes resonate with our audience.

Human resources:

- As an HR director, I want to extract key qualification data from incoming CVs so that I can screen candidates more efficiently while reducing unconscious bias.
- As an onboarding specialist, I want to automatically generate personalized welcome packets so that I can ensure new hires feel valued while maintaining consistency in information delivery.

Customer support:

- As a support team lead, I want to identify recurring customer issues from support tickets so that I can develop proactive solutions and reduce ticket volume.
- As a customer service representative, I want to access relevant product information while on calls so that I can resolve issues on the first contact without transferring customers between departments.

Sales:

- As a sales development representative, I want to receive notifications about prospect interactions with our content so that I can reach out at moments of highest interest.
- As a sales director, I want to visualize my team's pipeline by stage and probability so that I can accurately forecast quarterly revenue and identify deals needing intervention.

Product development

- As a product manager, I want to categorize and prioritize feature requests from multiple channels so that I can make data-driven decisions about our development roadmap.
- As a UX designer, I want to analyse user journey recordings by demographic segments so that I can identify where different user types encounter friction in our application.

Finance:

- As a financial analyst, I want to automatically flag unusual spending patterns so that I can investigate potential issues before they impact our monthly close process.
- As an accounts receivable specialist, I want to predict which invoices are likely to be paid late so that I can proactively manage cash flow and prioritize collection efforts.

Notice how effective user stories:

- clearly identify the specific role (who);
- articulate the exact action or capability needed (what);
- explain the tangible business outcome or value (why);
- avoid technical implementation details (how it should be built); and
- are specific enough to guide development but broad enough to allow creative solutions.

Of course, if we are going to build a better brain to power your new AI nervous system, it does not make sense to build a whole brain that just does one thing. The power of a digital twin of your organization in AI form is that it can tackle many, but the right types of, problems. For this, we have to decide what kind of brain we want to build. What kind of problems is it built to solve? For this we have to prioritize.

Prioritization methods for user stories

Once you have gathered your user stories, the next challenge is deciding which ones to tackle first. Here are several frameworks I have found particularly useful.

T-shirt sizing

This is my go-to method when working with cross-functional teams who may not all speak the same technical language. The beauty of T-shirt sizing is its simplicity: everyone understands what S, M, L and XL mean conceptually.

The process is straightforward: gather your stakeholders in a room (or on Zoom), present each user story, and have everyone vote on its size. This is not about implementation complexity; it is about the relative effort required compared to other stories.

- S – small: quick wins that can be implemented with minimal effort.
- M – medium: requires noticeable effort but still manageable.
- L – large: significant undertaking requiring substantial resources.
- XL – extra large: major projects that might need to be broken down further.

Where this method shines is in creating shared understanding. When the marketing director sees that the engineering lead rated something as 'XL' while they thought it was 'S', it sparks exactly the conversation you need to have before committing resources.

Effort/impact matrix

This is where we get more strategic. Plot your user stories on a 2×2 matrix with 'Effort Required' on one axis and 'Potential Impact' on the other. This creates four quadrants that guide your prioritization:

1. Quick wins (low effort, high impact): these should be your first priorities, they give you the most bang for your buck.
2. Major projects (high effort, high impact): these require significant investment but deliver substantial returns, plan these carefully.

3 Fill-ins (low effort, low impact): these can be addressed when resources are available or bundled with other work.

4 Thankless tasks (high effort, low impact): seriously question whether these should be done at all.

I have found this approach particularly effective when presenting to leadership teams. The visual nature of the matrix makes it immediately clear why certain initiatives should take precedence over others.

Pain/payoff analysis

Sometimes the most important metric is not effort but pain. How much is this problem actively hurting your organization right now? In a pain/payoff matrix, you evaluate each user story based on:

- Current pain level: how much is this issue costing us in time, money, missed opportunities or team frustration?
- Potential payoff: how valuable would solving this problem be?

This approach tends to surface the urgent versus important distinction that is crucial for sustainable transformation. High pain/high payoff items become obvious priorities, while low pain/low payoff items can often be eliminated from your backlog entirely.

What I appreciate about this method is how it centres the human experience. We are not just talking about abstract 'business value' – we are acknowledging real friction points that teams experience every day.

Whichever method you choose, the key is consistency. Pick one framework and apply it rigorously across all your user stories. This creates the transparency and trust necessary for teams to rally behind your prioritization decisions. Once you have identified your user stories and prioritized them, you are ready for step three in our process, which is to turn your collection of stories into broader problem statements to solve for.

How might we…

Turning user stories into problem statements

Prioritizing which stories to focus on – the good/fast/cheap dichotomy

My friend Jack introduced me to a simple paradigm early in my agency career. We were working on a client brief for Coca-Cola, trying to create a digital experience that was going to be 'the next big thing in entertainment' (spoiler: it was not). The client was on our backs about costs and Jack casually told me to speak to them – my job as the 'suit' in this scenario. They could only pick two.

'Pick two? Which two?' I asked. Day drinking was common in this particular office, but even by that standard it would have been early. Jack just smiled. 'Ask them: do they want it good, fast, or cheap? They can have any two, but not all three.'

Good. Fast. Cheap. Pick two. This simple Venn diagram should be taught in business schools around the world as the first rule of business. Most problems can be solved faster, cheaper or better – but rarely all at once. The skill is knowing which two matter most.

The thing that makes a business or organization stand out is when you can not only do it as well as the competition but better or faster. But it is very, very rare to do something better, faster and cheaper than the competition. Usually you only get to pick two.

The AI Difference: can you pick three?

If AI has disrupted anything so far, it may be this paradigm. When human capital can be replaced by AI capital, you can begin to have something better, faster and cheaper than the old way of doing things. AI is already showing us that, with near-equal quality, there are certain domains in which a 'narrow AI' application powered by LLMs (Large Language Models, see Chapter 1) can compete with the human equivalent quality (goodness) at much lower cost, or deliver the same results at the same cost but a lot faster.

Google's 2020 research noted that its latest neural machine translation reduced translation errors by an average of 60 per cent[6] compared to its previous phrase-based system, bringing translation quality to 85-95 per cent of human-level quality depending on the language pair.

JP Morgan's COIN (Contract Intelligence) program accomplishes in seconds what previously took legal experts 360,000 hours annually.[7] The system reviews commercial loan agreements with fewer errors than human lawyers.

AI writing assistants like Jasper and Copy.ai now produce marketing copy that, in A/B testing reported by HubSpot,[8] achieved click-through rates within 95–98 per cent of human-written content for certain formats like email subject lines and social media ads.

According to Gartner,[9] organizations implementing AI in customer service have seen resolution rates improve by 25 per cent and handling times decrease by 40 per cent. IBM reported that its Watson Assistant resolves 70 per cent of customer enquiries without human intervention, with satisfaction scores comparable to human agents.[10]

It is worth noting that these tools and systems are all forms of what we might call 'narrow AI'. Unlike general-purpose AI systems like ChatGPT or Claude, narrow AIs are specifically designed and optimized for particular tasks or domains. Here are some notable examples:

---

[6]https://slator.com/resources/how-accurate-is-google-translate/

[7]www.independent.co.uk/news/business/news/jp-morgan-software-lawyers-coin-contract-intelligence-parsing-financial-deals-seconds-legal-working-hours-360000-a7603256.html

[8]HubSpot (2023) 'AI copy A/B testing benchmarks'. Available at: https://research.hubspot.com

[9]Gartner (2023) 'Customer service and support: the state of generative AI'. Available at: www.gartner.com/en/customer-service-support/insights/generative-ai

[10]IBM (2023) 'Watson Assistant: client outcomes and benchmarks'. Available at: www.ibm.com/watsonx/assistant

- **Napkin AI** specializes in converting rough sketches and text descriptions into polished diagrams and flowcharts. While ChatGPT can describe how to create a diagram, Napkin AI actually generates the visual assets with proper formatting and design principles.
- **Harvey AI**, built specifically for legal professionals, excels at legal research, contract analysis and case law interpretation. It understands legal terminology, precedents and jurisdictional nuances that general AIs might miss or misinterpret.
- **Gamma**, focused exclusively on presentation creation, transforms basic content outlines into professionally designed presentations with appropriate visual hierarchy, animations and styling that would take significant manual effort in PowerPoint.
- **Midjourney** specializes in generating high-quality images from text descriptions, with particular strength in artistic styles and compositions that general AIs cannot match in visual quality or aesthetic coherence.
- **GitHub Copilot**, trained specifically on code repositories to assist software developers, it understands programming languages, design patterns, and best practices at a depth that allows it to suggest entire functions and implementations rather than just syntax help.

Most of the AIs we have in the world today have been trained to do certain tasks and processes better than others. You cannot pick up Jasper and ask it to do contract intelligence, or vice versa have JP Morgan's COIN write you a banger of a TikTok script (but I would love to see it try!).

Why narrow AIs often outperform general AIs

These specialized systems outperform general-purpose AIs like ChatGPT in their domains because they are:

- trained on domain-specific datasets that provide deeper context and understanding;
- optimized for specific output formats and quality standards relevant to their field;
- fine-tuned with feedback from professionals in those specific domains; and
- often combined with specialized tools or rendering capabilities beyond text generation.

These narrow AIs are good examples we can use as a proxy for the kind of new AI brain you might build in your organization or team. They each exemplify a way of doing work humans were doing before but faster, better or cheaper, freeing up human capital to work on more full-stack problems (see Chapter 8 on full stack skills).

So how do we take the problems we have identified in our user stories and decide what kind of AI brain we want to build? For this, I like to use the 'how might we…' statement.

Improvizational innovation

If you have worked in any corporate team or business for long enough you are likely to encounter the dreaded 'away day'. You know the kind of thing – trust falls with Sheila from Accounting or cocktail flaming with Derek from Finance. One of the often loved or loathed activities of such days 'away' is improv. Improvizational comedy relies on a core concept known as the 'Yes, and…' approach.

The 'how might we' (HMW) statement is essentially the business equivalent of improvizational theatre's 'Yes, and…' approach. Both create an environment where creativity flourishes by transforming constraints into possibilities.

'How might we' statements: business improv in action

In improvizational theatre, performers use the 'Yes, and…' technique to accept whatever situation is presented and then build upon it. There is no blocking, no negation, only acceptance and expansion. This creates a collaborative environment where surprising and innovative scenarios emerge. Similarly, 'how might we' statements transform business challenges from obstacles into invitations for creativity:

- Reframing problems as opportunities: just as improv actors turn unexpected suggestions into compelling scenes, HMW statements turn business problems into exciting innovation opportunities.
- Creating psychological safety: improv works because performers feel safe to contribute without judgement. HMW statements create this same safety in business settings by suggesting possibilities rather than demanding solutions.
- Collaborative building: in improv, each performer builds on what came before. HMW sessions encourage teams to build on each other's ideas rather than competing or critiquing.

Consider how these approaches compare:

Conventional business approach	**'How might we' (improv) approach**
'We need to reduce customer service costs.'	'How might we make customer service more efficient while improving satisfaction?'
'Our competitors are beating us on price.'	'How might we create value that makes price less relevant?'
'Compliance requirements are slowing us down.'	'How might we turn compliance into a competitive advantage?'

The magic of both improv and HMW statements lies in their ability to engage collective creativity by opening possibilities rather than narrowing them. They shift teams from reactive problem-solving to proactive opportunity-seeking.

Try this exercise: Next time your team faces a challenge, frame it as an improv scene. Start with 'How might we…' and watch how the energy in the room shifts from resignation to possibility. Have everyone build on ideas with 'Yes, and…' rather than 'No, but…' and notice how much further your thinking goes.

Faster

How might we do what we already do today but substantially faster than we do it today?

- What is one task you do every day, week, month or quarter that takes you more time than you wish it did?

This is a great starter question to ask yourself and your teams to start unearthing AI use cases.

Cheaper

How might we do what we already do today but do it substantially cheaper than we do it today?

- What is one area that is costing us too much money for the benefit it provides?

What is one area we are not acting on now because cost is a fear or blocker, but could pay off in the long run?

Better

How might we change what we already do today to make it substantially better?

- What is one thing we have been wishing we could do before but we do not have the expertise for?
- What is a skill set we are missing today to improve our quality of output?

Key takeaways

- Structure beats enthusiasm. Move from user stories to specs before tools and vendors.
- Design for incentives – clarify objectives versus reward functions so the system optimizes the right thing.
- Prioritize visibly – use one method consistently and defend why.
- Precision in language upstream yields better outputs downstream.
- Start with narrow wins, then generalize patterns.

Questions for reflection

1. What are the three highest-value user stories on your board right now, and why?
2. Where are incentives misaligned today and how will that distort AI behaviour if left unaddressed?

3. Which prioritization framework will you commit to, and who is the tiebreaker when scores disagree?
4. What spec would you hand an engineer tomorrow for one user story? What is missing?
5. Where can you run a low-risk pilot to validate assumptions within two weeks?

PART TWO

THE GUT

4

The AI ethics problem and putting the human in the loop

The second brain we forgot about

For most of history, the gut was treated as plumbing – essential, sometimes troublesome, but separate from how we think and feel. By the early twentieth century, researchers had catalogued much of the microbial world, but what of its significance for behaviour and decision-making? Still unclear.

Then in 1998, Michael Gershon's *The Second Brain*[1] popularized something pivotal: the gut has its own network of neurons – the enteric nervous system – that can operate independently from the brain. What we now call the gut–brain axis helps explain why gut health correlates with mood, stress responses, and even symptoms in conditions like Crohn's and IBS.

So why start here in a chapter on AI ethics? Because the gut–brain relationship is actually a perfect metaphor for how organizations should use AI. The 'brain' (your models, data and infrastructure) does powerful

[1]Gershon, M. (1999) *The Second Brain: The Scientific Basis of Gut Instinct and a Groundbreaking New Understanding of Nervous Disorders of the Stomach & Intestine.* Harper Collins.

computation. But without a 'gut' (shared principles, instincts and guardrails), that power can misfire. We notice our biological gut most when something's off – similarly, you only feel the absence of ethical instinct when a system crosses a line.

As your AI 'brain' takes on more decisions, you need clear boundaries for what it may and may not do. That's the work of developing an AI gut instinct – equipping teams with reflexes that make the right choice the easy choice, especially under pressure.

This chapter builds that instinct in two moves. First, we ground your program in a practical question that cuts through all the complexity: where should humans sit in the loop for each use case? Then, we expand to a simple, five-pillar ethics framework you can apply at speed. Taken together, these give you a repeatable way to act with confidence.

AI ethics: the human in the loop

My wife tried for several years to be a vegetarian. It wasn't that she had a hard moral code about eating animals or didn't care for meat – she had grown up on a relatively strict palette of chicken nuggets and, if feeling exotic, a spaghetti bolognese.

When we were visiting New York City for a work trip we found ourselves in a brightly lit diner at god-awful-o'clock in the morning fighting jet lag but soothing our souls with endless amounts of drip coffee. I ordered my usual bacon (crispy), eggs (scrambled) and toast (brown). Our cheery server, which seems to be the hallmark of American diner culture where tipping still counts for something, turned to take my wife's order, who I assumed was deliberating between porridge or . . . another kind of porridge. 'I'll have the pancakes with a side of bacon.' And like that – the ethical experiment ended. Sometimes all it takes is a side of bacon.

The rules we set ourselves

Most of us don't walk around thinking about 'ethics' every day. The rules by which we live our lives are deep set, long developed and experienced automatically. Whether placed there in our youth by parents or carers who set 'this is how we do things in this house' or by the moral order instilled by a faith tradition, football team or education system – most of us operate through life making judgements about right or wrong relatively on autopilot.

Then of course there are circumstances, revelations or life events that cause us to adjust our moral order. Perhaps a conversion experience like my own during a ninth grade youth group, or the first time you encounter poverty on the streets, or someone shows you how those chicken nuggets were made. Or maybe like the first time you asked ChatGPT for advice.

As we think about how AI comes into our workplaces, families and communities, more and more of us are pausing for thought. Just because AI *can* write that essay, make that calculation, write that code, should we allow it to do so?

Technology has a funny way of shifting the moral order – making us rethink the way we do things. Take the explosive popularity of the new class of weight loss drugs sweeping the Western world. On the one hand, they promise respite from disease and the medical burden on our public healthcare systems as a result. On the other, patients without sufficient insurance or where government healthcare places restitutions on access means only those who can afford them are able to benefit.

Recent data shows that GLP-1 receptor agonists have seen explosive adoption, with global prescriptions increasing by over 300 per cent between 2020 and 2023.[2] Clinical trials demonstrate significant health benefits –

[2]www.rheumatologyadvisor.com/news/glp-1-receptor-agonist-dispensing-up-from-2020-to-2023-for-teens-young-adults/

patients lose an average of 15–20 per cent of their body weight, and see meaningful improvements in cardiovascular health, blood sugar control, and reduced risk of diabetes complications. Yet this efficacy has created a profound moral dilemma. In the United States, these medications can cost $900–$1,300 per month without insurance coverage. While those with comprehensive insurance or personal wealth can access life-changing treatment, many who would benefit most – those with obesity-related health conditions, limited incomes and inadequate insurance – simply cannot afford them. Public health systems in many countries are struggling with whether and how to provide coverage, often implementing strict eligibility criteria that exclude patients who could benefit. We face a growing divide – a technology exists that can dramatically improve health outcomes, but access is determined not by medical need but by ability to pay.

This is the exact tension we will encounter with AI – powerful tools that could transform outcomes, but whose benefits may accrue only to those with resources to deploy them, and some pretty heavy potential downsides for those that choose not to pick them up at all, even when the cost of doing so goes to zero.

As laid out in the previous chapters, if we build a better AI brain for our teams and organization then maybe AI too can take the hard work out of shifting our unnecessary administrative pounds and kilos. However, if we don't learn to rewire our gut instincts for what we should and shouldn't be using AI for, then we are headed for some difficult times ahead.

AI ethics: understanding good vs not bad

Why talk about AI ethics?

AI ethics is a topic in and of itself, but it's also a topic that is often confuse. AI ethics isn't saying that AI has an ethic or that there is such a thing as an AI ethic. What we're actually talking about is the use of AI by humans, and how do we do that ethically? It's important to start with that first distinction.

Much like the debate that has raged since the days of Oppenheimer and the Manhattan Project around how nuclear weapons were developed, there is a use of this technology for good and a use of this technology for bad, and we need to be clear about the distinction between the two.

AI as tool, throne, or weapon

First, let's establish what AI is, and what it's not. A quick tour through YouTube or the average business conference will turn up the often-overused phrase 'AI is just a tool' – and I have some time for that argument, but it's a little reductive – but let's go with it for a minute.

Tools can of course be neutral. The chair that I'm sat on as I sit here writing this chapter is a function of physics and ergonomics to keep me off the ground – it's a tool, is neutral. So long as I use it in that way it's achieving its aim as a tool. It's completely benign. It has no morals. It doesn't care whether I'm sat on it fully or sat on it to the side. It doesn't care if I pick it up and move it to the left or to the right. And to everyone else around me, it doesn't really matter how I'm sat on the chair either.

But the minute that I pick up this chair and decide to throw it across the room, or smack you around the head with it, suddenly it takes on a whole other meaning. It's no longer just its own thing, because I have enacted some human agency on it. It's gone from being a tool to a weapon.

But what's even more challenging is that, if you pick up a chair and put it on a stage in a banqueting hall, and then we sit someone down on it – well, we go from calling it a chair to calling it something more like a throne, and we put someone on that throne.

The challenge that AI presents to us is that it may be more than just a tool that we can use and wield, much like a weapon, in a similar way to what we have seen with the power of nuclear armament. But we can also – unlike nukes – use it to take on the position of the throne in our lives. It could be the thing that we begin to rely upon, as a crutch, or even as something to defend ourselves with or to make progress with in the way that a chair in a chariot makes progress. But this may become the object of our knowledge, the object of our worship, and potentially even the object of our government. And that's why we have to treat it with particular caution. So yes, AI is just a tool. But the minute that we as humans begin to act upon it, it takes on very different connotations, and a very different role in our lives.

Growing minds: how AIs are made

The other challenge to the tool argument is that tools are designed, built and manufactured from parts we choose. Modern AI systems however aren't assembled like traditional software, or built like the chair I'm sat on. They're not built line by line with predictable, traceable behaviours – in fact, often we don't even know the parts they are made of. Large Language Models today aren't built . . . instead, they're **grown**.

Consider the difference. When you build something – a house, a car, furniture – you know exactly what materials went where. You can trace every component to its source. If something breaks, you know where to look and how to fix it. Growing something is fundamentally different. When you plant a seed, you know generally what kind of plant you'll get. You understand what it needs – soil, water, sunlight. You can guide its growth with careful tending. But you cannot predict exactly which way each branch will grow, how many leaves will sprout, or the precise pattern of veins in each leaf.

This is how AI models develop. We provide the 'DNA' – the training data, the architecture, the optimization algorithms. We create the conditions for growth – the computational resources, the training procedures, the reward signals. But the specific patterns that emerge, the exact ways the model learns to solve problems, the particular associations it forms – these arise through a process closer to organic development than mechanical assembly.

When OpenAI trains GPT, when Google grows Gemini, when Anthropic cultivates Claude, they start with fundamental building blocks and allow complex behaviours to emerge through exposure to vast amounts of data and iterative refinement. The final model contains billions or trillions of parameters, forming patterns that even the creators cannot fully map or predict in advance. This has profound implications for AI ethics. You can audit code. You can review blueprints. You can test mechanisms. But how do you govern something that was grown rather than built? How do you ensure ethical behaviour in a system whose internal representations emerged rather than being explicitly programmed?

The answer lies in two critical intervention points – *what you feed it during growth* (the training data and process), and *how you guide it after growth* (the system prompts and guardrails). These become the ethical foundation – the DNA and the environment – that shape how AI systems behave when deployed in your organization.

Eliezer Yudkowsky's work on AI safety[3] explores this phenomenon. AIs aren't simply built like Lego blocks, where each parameter is well known, constructed with design intent, and assembled to a set of instructions. It's more like growing a mind or an organism. We know that a certain DNA sequence might produce a certain plant, animal or human. But exactly how that organism will look and behave isn't determined until it's fully grown. The same applies to how these models are trained. All the component parts – the DNA, the genome sequencing, the pieces that make you you and me me – could be mapped and

[3]Yudkowsky, E. (2008) 'Artificial intelligence as a positive and negative factor in global risk', in Bostrom, N. and Ćirković, M. (eds) *Global Catastrophic Risks*. Oxford: Oxford Univerity Press.

known at some point. Yet there's a real challenge: just because you know what I look like, how I sound, and what my upbringing has been like, you still don't know what I am about to say.

Every aloe vera plant is different. You can picture one in your mind. We know how the cells photosynthesize. We know the building blocks of life that go into growing it. But every plant is unique, every spine on a cactus, every snowflake – grown in an organic fashion. AIs are grown this way too.

Ethical training: the DNA of AI behaviour

One of the core things that goes into that growing is a set of ethical rules and boundaries, guidance and symbology, guided by the system-prompting of the AI makers and coupled with the training data that the models have been trained on. It is these two big component parts that give these different AIs different ethical training.

We see, in particular, with models that are being grown at the moment, that they take on the ethical stances of their creators. A great challenge was raised in early 2024 when the emergence of the DeepSeek R1 model from a company in China began to demonstrate that it had similar levels of capability to the likes of o1, the model that, at the time, was most advanced from OpenAI's ChatGPT team.[4]

What was particularly interesting about this was that we found that when using models like R1, and asking it to exhibit behaviours that might be challenging to the Chinese government, or to get them to say things that might be contrary to what the CCP might deem to be acceptable speech – they pushed back. Many examples were cited at the time of trying to ask the models to give an explanation of what happened in Tiananmen Square, or what the

[4]www.wired.com/story/deepseek-china-model-ai/

CCP's views were on the one-child policy, but would come back with models either giving glowing reviews of what's going on in China, or simply refusing to answer.

It is this ethical training that is integrated at the training phase of these models and then guided through the system prompts.

System prompts: the hidden ethical guidance

What is the system prompt? Well you know when you load up ChatGPT, Gemini or Claude and type in your prompt – that's not all the model sees. The model is guided, and it's guided by the 'system prompt' – written, crafted and edited over time by the model creator. Every time you send a piece of information to an AI model, you send with it not only your intent from your own prompting, maybe some additional context that you've attached along the way – like a document you have attached or some text you have pasted in – but behind the scenes, the system prompt – which is written by the companies that design the models – is also being sent to the model to guide it on how to behave and what it should and shouldn't do.

These system prompts are, in some cases, very transparently published by the likes of Anthropic.[5] Or they can be inferred by asking the models themselves to give you more information about how they are guided and how they are to behave. In either case, these prompts – which can span many pages – are doing the act of essentially guiding the model to behave how you want it to behave at the time in which you send the prompt to it.

It is this prompting that also contains ethical training data – not just the training that is in the model at the time that it is grown through the content that is seen on the internet or whatever the model is trained upon, but also the content that is sent to it by those who would write these prompts. These system

[5]Anthropic (2024) 'System prompt and constitutional AI overview'. Available at: www.anthropic.com/news/constitutional-ai

prompts define organizational personality and ethical guidelines, include fine-tuning on company data including internal documents and communication patterns, and incorporate behavioural alignment through reinforcement learning from human feedback (RLHF) or reinforcement learning from AI feedback (RLAIF) using organizational values.

The Guardrails problem: early failures and responses

We've seen in the early days of some of these models as they've been released that without this guided prompting, it's been very easy to get around certain use cases that the makers of the models would be less than happy to create. For example, in the early days of the Gemini model being released by Google for image generation, prompters were able to create images of rather ethnically diverse and racially diverse Nazis in Nazi uniforms and costumes. Clearly not something that the creators at Google had intended, nor that anyone would like to see being shared on the internet. But it was possible nonetheless, simply because the guardrails of how that model should behave were not put in place.

Now, some might argue (and indeed have, by the likes of Elon Musk and Grok, and in the creation of their models by xAI) that we should – in the true freedom of speech model exhibited in Western democracies, and particularly in the United States – allow anyone to create anything with these models in the same way that we wouldn't allow journalists to be censored – or political figures be restricted on what they can and can't say. That push for freedom of speech continues to shape the arguments made by the model makers themselves. And so many of the model makers have since the early stages of 2023 begun to introduce more and more controls and parameters into their system prompts. And these prompts now begin to reflect back certain ethical stances of those creators. You can't ask a model today to give you an exegesis on the devil if it was deemed to be too scary for a child who might be consuming the content. We have controls now that protect children in the use of some of these models through parental controls. Inside many of the model prompts, there are controls to limit the ability of model users to ask for things like information on how to enrich uranium or create a bioweapon – and I'm very glad that those controls are there. But these are all ethical choices by the model makers. And we've seen that many will try and get around them cunningly, perhaps even by just switching the language in which they are prompting to get the model to respond differently.

Acknowledging different ethical frameworks

We have to acknowledge that different AIs do have different ethical training, that they are modelled after their creators, and that how we actually use them matters deeply. This is the field of AI ethics that we need to unpack if we are going to make our organizations able to leverage these models soundly.

AI for Good vs AI for not bad

Now we need to separate out what we actually mean by ethics in this context. My friend Ru Blackman frames this brilliantly in his book *Ethical Machines*,[6] distinguishing between two categories of AI ethics: AI for good and AI for not bad.

---

[6]Blackman, R. (2022) *Ethical Machines: Your Concise Guide to Totally Unbiased, Transparent, and Respectful AI*. New York: McGraw-Hill.

AI for good: the macro concerns

The 'AI for good' crowd are mostly worried about things like sustainability. How sustainable are these models that use a lot of water, energy and computing power? We're worried about safety – how safe are they to actually use? Are they ripping our data? Are they doing dangerous stuff? And there's this whole area of model control – can we lock them down so they don't publish themselves on the web and replicate a million times and take over the energy grid? These are existential threats, essentially.

Many of these issues are, frankly, more hyperbole than they are real at the minute. While they're important concerns that need attention at the governmental and societal level, they're not the daily ethical challenges most of us face when implementing AI in our organizations.

AI for not bad: where we live every day

The bit that I think we should be more concerned about is the AI for not bad. This is where it comes to what we do ourselves personally, what we choose to do internally within the business, and what we choose to work with externally – with clients, with customers and with society. These 'not bad' use cases are more about:

- How does this AI usage affect the business?
- How does it affect the way that we perform as a business?
- How does it affect you all as individuals?
- What do we do that affects you individually?
- How does it affect the customers and clients that we work with, and how does it affect our other stakeholders – the public, the media, the government, other people that we have to deal with?

This is the stuff that really matters for most of us in our daily lives. This is where ethics becomes practical rather than philosophical.

The central question: Where is the human in the loop?

When we talk about AI ethics in organizations, it can feel overwhelming. Privacy, security, trust, transparency, accountability, sustainability – the list goes on and sometimes it feels like we need a PhD in philosophy just to deploy a chatbot. But there's one question that cuts through all of this complexity: Where is the human in the loop?

This isn't just an academic exercise. When your team starts implementing AI solutions – and they will, because the competitive pressure is too great to ignore – this question becomes the cornerstone of responsible deployment.

The three positions: in, on, or out of the loop

Think of any AI system you're already using. Your spam filter, for example. Where are you in that loop? When you get something filtered into your spam folder by a phishing detector, where are you in the loop in that moment? Are you in the loop, on the loop or out of the loop?

You're *out of the loop*. You're not looking at every one of those things – it's just happening in the background. Most of the time it works. Not all the time, as we've seen, but most of the time. But when an AI auto-writes you a reply – perhaps if you're using Gemini in your personal Google email and it auto-writes you a reply but doesn't send it for you – you are *on the loop*. You are looking at this reply and then choosing what to do with it. And for most of us, when we write our emails, we're *in the loop*. We're the ones writing the email, at least for now.

The loop framework in practice

This loop question comes up everywhere. Every single day.

An AI scans your CRM and recommends which deals to prioritize. Another decides who gets your outreach emails based on engagement patterns. A third reviews customer support tickets and routes them without human eyes ever seeing the initial triage. Where are you in those loops?

Let me give you an example that should make you uncomfortable. Imagine your HR team starts using AI to analyse everyone's one-to-one meeting recordings on Teams. The AI listens for tone, politeness markers and engagement signals. Then it generates a 'collaboration score' that feeds into bonus calculations. Your raise depends partly on how nice you sounded to your manager in those supposedly private check-ins. Where would you want to be in that loop? (For the record, they don't do that. Don't worry. They're not doing that yet. But someone, somewhere, is probably already building it.)

The technology doesn't care about the ethics. We do. Which means every time we introduce these systems, we have to ask ourselves: Where will the human be in the loop?

Let's work through some real scenarios you're probably already facing.

Editorial screening

You're a publisher receiving hundreds of unsolicited manuscript proposals every month. You build an AI agent to screen them. It checks whether the writing is competent, whether the proposal follows your guidelines, whether it's from an author you've worked with before. You train it on successful proposals from the past five years. You add rules about word count, genre fit, market viability.

Here's the question: Will you review everything this agent does? Will you look at every proposal it rejects, every one it flags as promising? Or will you trust it to handle the obvious nos – the ones that are clearly off-brand or incomplete – while you focus your human attention on the maybes and the promising ones?

There's no obviously right answer here. If you're in the loop on everything, you've built an assistant, not an agent. You're still doing most of the work. If you're out of the loop entirely, you're trusting an AI to make subjective judgement calls about art and commercial potential. That's . . . a choice.

Most organizations end up on the loop – reviewing batches, spot-checking the AI's work, adjusting parameters when it gets things wrong. But even that's a deliberate positioning. You're choosing which criteria matter enough for human judgement and which can be automated away.

Social media management

Your marketing team is drowning. You need consistent social presence across three platforms, posting daily, engaging with trends, maintaining brand voice. Someone suggests using AI to generate a month's worth of posts in an afternoon.

You try it. The AI churns out perfectly adequate content. Nothing brilliant, nothing terrible. It hits your brand guidelines, uses appropriate hashtags, varies the format. It would take your team two weeks to produce what the AI created in twenty minutes.

So are you reviewing every single post before it goes out? That's being in the loop – you're still the bottleneck, just with better first drafts. Are you reviewing batches of ten at a time, making edits, then trusting the AI to generate similar quality? That's being on the loop – you're supervising, not creating. Or are you setting up the agent with clear parameters and letting it post automatically, only checking in when something gets flagged? That's being out of the loop – you're monitoring outcomes, not reviewing inputs.

Different organizations will make different choices here. A financial services firm might never go out of the loop on public communications – the regulatory and reputational risks are too high. A consumer brand with a more casual voice might be comfortable being on the loop. A personal brand might stay firmly in the loop because authenticity is the entire value proposition.

The point isn't that one approach is right. The point is that you have to choose consciously, not drift into automation by default.

Meeting summaries and action items

This one's already happening in most organizations. AI joins your meetings, takes notes, generates summaries, extracts action items. It's remarkably good at this. Often better than the distracted human who was also trying to participate in the discussion. But here's where it gets interesting. When the AI assigns an action item to someone, are you reviewing that assignment? When it decides something is high priority versus low priority, are you checking its work? When it summarizes a nuanced discussion into three bullet points, are you making sure nothing important got lost?

Most people are out of the loop on this already. The AI sends the summary, everyone trusts it, work proceeds based on potentially flawed interpretations. We've collectively decided that the efficiency gains outweigh the risk of misunderstandings. Maybe that's fine for routine team meetings. But what about strategic planning sessions? Client negotiations? Performance reviews? Same tool, same technology, very different stakes.

This is what I mean about the loop framework being practical. It's not a philosophical question – it's a decision you're making dozens of times as you deploy these tools. In some contexts, you need to be in the loop. In others, on the loop is sufficient. In others still, being out of the loop is the whole point. So where are we in the loop – in, on or out? This is one of the simplest ethics questions you can ask about AI. It's also one of the most crucial.

Different organizations will need different frameworks as AI becomes more sophisticated and autonomous. In the next chapter, we'll explore specific frameworks like the Open Voice Trust Mark[7] – how they actually work in practice, what implementing them looks like day-to-day, how they help you make these loop decisions systematically rather than ad hoc.

---

[7]Open Voice Network (2022) 'Open Voice Trust Mark'. Linux Foundation. Available at: https://openvoicenetwork.org/

But whatever framework you choose, whatever policies you write, whatever training you roll out, it should always come back to this central question: Where is the human in the loop? And more importantly: did we choose that position intentionally, or did we just drift there because the technology made it easy?

AI ethics isn't about the AI – it's about us

It's about the choices we make, the boundaries we set, and the gut instinct we develop to navigate an increasingly AI-augmented world. The question isn't whether AI will transform work and society – it will. The question is whether we'll shape that transformation thoughtfully, with clear ethical frameworks and strong organizational gut instincts, or whether we'll let it shape us by default.

Key takeaways

- **AI systems inherit ethical frameworks from their creators.** Through training data, system prompts and reinforcement learning, AI models reflect the values and priorities of those who build them. Understanding this helps us evaluate which models align with our organizational values.
- **System prompts are the invisible ethical layer.** The instructions given to AI models at runtime shape their behaviour as much as their training data. These prompts encode organizational personality, ethical guidelines and behavioural boundaries.
- **AI ethics has two distinct domains.** 'AI for good' addresses macro concerns like sustainability and existential risks, while 'AI for not bad' focuses on practical, daily ethical challenges in business contexts. Most organizations need to focus primarily on the latter.

- **The central ethical question is about human positioning.** Where is the human in the loop – in, on or out? This simple framework cuts through complexity and provides a practical lens for evaluating any AI implementation.
- **Different use cases require different loop positions.** There's no one-size-fits-all answer. Spam filtering might justify humans being out of the loop, while HR decisions require humans firmly in the loop. The key is making intentional choices.
- **Guardrails evolve through failure.** Early AI mishaps (like Google Gemini's diverse Nazi images) demonstrate why ethical boundaries matter. Model makers continuously refine these controls, but organizations must still establish their own ethical frameworks.
- **Ethics isn't about the AI – it's about us.** The technology itself is neutral. What matters are the choices we make about how to deploy it, what boundaries we set, and how we maintain human agency in increasingly automated systems.

Questions for reflection

1. What are the three most significant AI applications currently in use (or being considered) in your organization? For each one, where is the human in the loop – in, on or out?
2. Can you identify any AI systems in your organization where humans have moved from 'in the loop' to 'on the loop' or 'out of the loop' without explicit discussion or decision-making? What prompted those shifts?
3. When you think about your organization's values and culture, which AI model providers seem most aligned with those values? What evidence supports your assessment?

4. Consider a recent decision in your organization that involved AI recommendations or outputs. How would that decision have been different if humans were positioned differently in the loop?
5. What are the highest-stakes decisions in your organization or department? What would it take for you to be comfortable with AI being 'out of the loop' for any of these decisions? Are there any where you'd never be comfortable with that?
6. How transparent is your organization about when and how AI is being used with external stakeholders (customers, clients, partners)? Should this transparency be different for different use cases?
7. Think about the system prompts or ethical guidelines your organization might create for AI use. What three non-negotiable principles would you include? What behaviours would you explicitly prohibit?
8. Rid Blackman distinguishes between 'AI for good' and 'AI for not bad'. Which category occupies more of your mental space when thinking about AI ethics? Should that balance change?
9. Can you recall a time when you felt uncomfortable about how AI was being used – either in your organization or elsewhere? What specifically triggered that discomfort? What does that tell you about your own ethical instincts?
10. If you had to explain to a new employee where your organization stands on AI ethics in two minutes, what would you say? Does your organization actually have a clear stance, or would this be difficult to articulate?

5

Developing AI gut instinct

The Oppenheimer moment: why responsibility matters

When I talk to leading researchers in the field of AI, they literally refer to this as their Oppenheimer moment. The comparison isn't about destruction, it's about responsibility. When Oppenheimer said 'Now I am become Death, destroyer of worlds" he wasn't just expressing regret about the bomb. He was acknowledging that scientists and technologists have a moral obligation that extends beyond the laboratory.

The tragedy of Oppenheimer wasn't that he created the bomb, it was that he convinced himself he bore no responsibility for how it was used. Oppenheimer convinced himself that just because he and his team created the nuclear bomb, he has no responsibility for its use. This abdication of responsibility, the notion that technology is morally neutral and developers bear no responsibility for its application, is precisely the trap we must avoid with AI.

AI won't destroy the world through mushroom clouds, but it will reshape work, decision-making and human agency in ways we're only beginning to understand. Like nuclear technology, it demands that we develop robust ethical frameworks, not because the technology is inherently evil, but because its power demands wisdom in application.

The Manhattan Project teaches us important lessons about accountability and transparency. After the nuclear age began, a movement emerged questioning the role of science and government, leading to deeper arguments about how government should direct science in socially responsible ways. This resulted in institutions like the Office of Technology Assessment in the USA, which provided Congress with information to make decisions about emerging technologies.

The US government defunded that office in 1995. Since then, some of the world's most influential technologies have been developed and implemented into the mainstream without systematic oversight – including the internet, social media and artificial intelligence. We're essentially flying blind, making the same mistakes Oppenheimer warned against.

But here's what the nuclear community got right that we can learn from: they developed frameworks for responsible development. Nuclear treaties rely on verification and disclosure. Scientists like Joseph Rotblat simply walked away from the Manhattan Project when he realized its true purpose, demonstrating that researchers can and should make ethical choices about their work. We need the same principled approach to AI. Not to stop progress, but to ensure it serves human flourishing rather than undermining it.

What nuclear governance can teach us about AI

Here is the thing about nuclear technology: it didn't destroy the world. Not because the bombs aren't powerful enough – they absolutely are. But because humanity, despite all our flaws, managed to build governance structures that made cooperation more rational than chaos.

The decades following Hiroshima and Nagasaki show us how it's possible to create frameworks for transformative technologies. Within twenty years of the first atomic bombs, the world established the 1968 Treaty on the Non-

Proliferation of Nuclear Weapons. The NPT didn't stop nuclear technology – it created something more valuable: a shared language that made responsible development possible. Think about what the treaty actually accomplished:

- **It gave us common definitions.** The NPT distinguished between nuclear-weapon states and non-nuclear-weapon states. Sounds simple, but this shared vocabulary enabled meaningful negotiation between rivals who wouldn't otherwise agree on anything.
- **It created verification mechanisms.** The International Atomic Energy Agency developed inspection protocols that allowed 'trust but verify' – a model that balanced national sovereignty with collective security. You didn't have to trust your rival's good intentions; you just had to trust the inspection process.
- **It acknowledged beneficial uses.** The treaty recognized that nuclear technology could serve humanity – medical isotopes, power generation, research – while establishing safeguards to prevent weaponization. It wasn't anti-technology; it was pro-responsibility.
- **It established consequences.** Clear penalties for violation, enforced imperfectly but meaningfully enough to shape behaviour.

These treaties worked not because they were perfect, but because they made cooperation rational even for competing powers. The Soviet Union and United States, locked in existential rivalry, could still agree on nuclear verification protocols. Why? Because the alternative – unconstrained proliferation – threatened everyone.

We need this same approach for AI. I'm not saying we need a single global AI treaty tomorrow – the technology landscape is different, more distributed, faster-moving. But we desperately need shared frameworks that make responsible development the path of least resistance. Here's what that looks like in practice:

- **Common terminology matters more than you think.** What counts as 'high-risk AI'? When is a system truly 'autonomous'? Without agreed definitions, regulation becomes arbitrary and compliance becomes expensive guesswork. Right now, we're flying blind because we can't even agree on what we're talking about.
- **Transparency standards that actually work.** Just as nuclear facilities submit to inspections, AI systems above certain capability thresholds need documentation that external auditors can review: not to steal intellectual property; to verify safety claims. The nuclear industry figured out how to do this while protecting legitimate secrets. So can we.
- **Impact assessment before deployment.** The nuclear industry uses probabilistic risk assessment to evaluate reactor safety before they flip the switch. AI needs equivalent frameworks for evaluating fairness, privacy and societal impact before deployment at scale, not after we discover problems in production.
- **Industry self-governance backed by regulation.** Nuclear power developed robust safety culture partly through industry bodies like the Institute of Nuclear Power Operations, which set standards exceeding legal minimums. AI needs similar professional standards that practitioners actually follow – not because lawyers force them to, but because it's how professionals behave.

The EU AI Act[1] represents the first major attempt at this kind of framework, creating risk categories and corresponding obligations. Whether it succeeds depends on whether it establishes shared language that works across borders, or fragments into incompatible national approaches that make responsible global development harder.

---

[1]EU (2025) The Artificial Intelligence Act. Available at: https://artificialintelligenceact.eu/

But here's what we can learn from the nuclear precedent: governance frameworks work best when they're built *with* technologists rather than imposed *on* them; when they acknowledge legitimate security and commercial interests while still requiring transparency; when they create positive incentives for compliance rather than just punishments for violation.

Most importantly, nuclear governance succeeded because leading scientists like Rotblat, Oppenheimer, and Szilard insisted that technical expertise carries moral responsibility. They didn't wait for governments to tell them to care – they claimed that responsibility themselves. We need AI researchers and practitioners to do the same. Not as a constraint on innovation, but as the foundation that makes sustained innovation possible. Because without that foundation – without shared frameworks and genuine accountability – we're just building more powerful systems without the wisdom to use them well. And history shows us exactly how that story ends.

So how do we build that wisdom into our organizations? How do we create practical frameworks that work in the real world, not just in policy documents? That's where the five pillars come in.

The five pillars of ethical AI

While 'where is the human in the loop' provides a practical framework for individual decisions, organizations need a more comprehensive approach to guide their overall AI strategy. Across industry, academia, and regulatory bodies, five core dimensions have emerged as the foundation of responsible AI practice.

These aren't my invention – they're the consensus view. Whether you're reading the EU AI Act, IEEE standards, or enterprise governance frameworks, you'll find these same themes. They've been pressure-tested across everything from early voice assistants to today's generative models, and they hold up because they address fundamental questions about power, trust and human dignity that don't change as the technology evolves.

I've applied this framework across roles – from founding Vixen Labs (a conversational AI agency acquired by House 337 in 2023), to advising on AI ethics at the Open Voice Network,[2] AI & Faith, and Christian Vision's Technology and Ethics Board, to leading AI transformation at scale. What makes it work isn't complexity – it is that each pillar maps to a simple gut-check question you can ask in the moment. The framework rests on five pillars, each addressing a crucial dimension of responsible AI use.

1. Privacy: the sanctity of the individual

Case study: Network Rail's AI CCTV pilot

In 2022, Network Rail tested AI-equipped CCTV across major UK stations. Documents later revealed[3] the system could infer demographics and even 'emotion' states, with talk of using insights to optimize ads. As a commuter and consultant, my instinctive 'gut check' here is privacy first – if passengers don't know what's being captured and why, trust collapses. Even if the intent is safety, mixing hazard detection with monetization crosses a line – unless governance is explicit, consent is meaningful, and the scope is tightly bounded with deletion standards and public reporting. That's why, in my programs, I default to data minimization, clear signage, DPO review and an opt-out where feasible. It's not anti-innovation; it's pro-legitimacy.

Privacy isn't just about compliance with GDPR or other regulations, though that's part of it. At a deeper level, it's about respecting that individuals – whether employees, customers or the public – have a right to control information about themselves. In practical terms, this means asking:

---

[2]Open Voice Network (2022) 'Open Voice Trust Mark'. Linux Foundation. Available at: https://openvoicenetwork.org

[3]www.standard.co.uk/news/london/network-rail-ai-cameras-train-stations-london-euston-waterloo-b1165407.html

- What data are we collecting through our AI systems, and do people know about it?
- How are we storing and protecting this data?
- Are we using personal data to train AI models, and if so, have we obtained appropriate consent?
- Can individuals access, correct, or delete information about them?

When the civil liberties group Big Brother Watch[4] revealed these details, public concern intensified. The organization argued that Network Rail had 'no right to deploy discredited emotion recognition technology against unwitting commuters' and warned that mixing safety measures with tools designed to maximize advertising revenue compromised passenger privacy. Network Rail denied analysing emotional data and said the demographic analysis component had already been discontinued, but the damage to trust was done.

The lesson isn't that AI surveillance is always wrong – it's that organizations must be transparent about what data they're collecting and why, and must have legitimate justifications that align with public expectations. Network Rail's safety justification for the cameras was widely accepted; the undisclosed emotion analysis for advertising purposes was not.

2. Transparency: truthfulness and integrity

Case study: Tesco's AI-shaped 'nudges' in Clubcard

When Tesco rolled out Clubcard Challenges to millions of shoppers, AI looked across past purchases to suggest personalized goals and timing. As a shopper and a strategist, my instinct is to welcome the efficiency while drawing a bright

[4]Big Brother Watch (2023) 'Emotion recognition in UK stations'. Available at: https://bigbrotherwatch.org.uk/

line on transparency and consent. If an AI suggests I wait a week because a healthier, lower-salt option will be on offer, that can be pro-customer.

But if those nudges start to mimic medical advice without clinical oversight, or bury trade-offs in small print, that trips my transparency wire. In programmes I run, we label AI-influenced offers, provide a clear 'why you're seeing this', and allow users to dial nudges up, down or off.

Transparency is about being honest, with yourself and others, about what your AI systems are doing and how they work. This doesn't mean you need to publish your source code or explain the mathematics of neural networks. It means people should understand, in plain language, when they're interacting with AI and how it's influencing decisions that affect them. In practice, this means:

- disclosing when content has been AI-generated;
- explaining how AI systems make decisions, especially when those decisions affect people's opportunities or outcomes;
- being honest about AI limitations and failure modes; and
- not using AI to deceive or manipulate.

The Albanian government's approach to AI offers a cautionary tale about the limits of transparency. In early 2025, Albania appointed the world's first AI-powered government official, an avatar named 'Alba' that would provide assistance to citizens through a government portal. Prime Minister Edi Rama presented this as a technological breakthrough that would make government services more accessible.[5]

The reaction was swift and scathing. Opposition figures called it a 'desperate gimmick' and accused Rama of turning Albania into a 'laughing stock'. Legal experts questioned the constitutional implications of an AI making

[5]www.aljazeera.com/news/2025/9/12/albania-appoints-ai-bot-minister-to-fight-corruption-in-world-first

governmental decisions. Critics argued that while AI assistance might be valuable, disguising it as a government minister was misleading and undermined democratic accountability.

When newsrooms piloted AI-assisted article drafts, the *Financial Times* publicly disclosed[6] AI involvement on experimental pages and published its internal AI principles, committing to human editorial control and clear labelling. I follow the same pattern in client work: label AI-influenced content, explain 'why you're seeing this,' and keep a human editor in the loop for publication. Transparency that people can understand beats technical dumps every time.

3. Inclusivity: equal dignity of all people

Case study: Gemini's 'synthetic inclusion' miss

In early 2025, Google paused people-image generation in Gemini after it produced racially diverse depictions of Nazis and other historically specific groups.[7] My instinct here is that intention mattered but outcome mattered more. Turning away from racist outputs is a good goal; erasing context and warping history isn't an acceptable side-effect. In practice, when I'm building generative systems, I pair bias-mitigation with rigorous context rules – if a request is historically bounded, the model must preserve that constraint or decline with a clear explanation. Inclusivity is not achieved by papering over the past; it's achieved by being truthful about it while widening representation where the context actually allows it. Inclusivity in AI isn't just about diversity in your training data, though that matters. It's about ensuring that your AI systems serve all people fairly, regardless of their background, identity or circumstances.

The challenge is that AI systems learn from historical data, and historical data reflects historical biases. If you train an AI hiring system on data from a

---

[6]https://aboutus.ft.com/careers/ft-blog/evolving-for-the-ai-era-how-the-financial-times-is

[7]www.theguardian.com/technology/2024/feb/22/google-pauses-ai-generated-images-of-people-after-ethnicity-criticism

company that historically hired mostly men for technical roles, the AI will learn to prefer male candidates. If you train a credit scoring system on data from a period when discriminatory lending practices were common, the AI will perpetuate those discriminatory patterns. Amazon learned this the hard way when it tried to use machine learning to screen job candidates.[8] The company wanted to increase diversity in hiring, but the training data it used – previous hires – wasn't particularly diverse. The AI system learned to penalize resumés that included words like 'women's' (as in 'women's chess club captain') and downgraded graduates of all-women colleges. Amazon scrapped the system.

The solution isn't to avoid AI in hiring, it's to be intentional about fairness from the start. This means:

- auditing training data for bias before using it;
- testing AI systems across different demographic groups to ensure fair outcomes;
- maintaining human oversight for decisions that significantly affect people's opportunities; and
- being willing to sacrifice some efficiency for fairness when the stakes are high.

4. Accountability: taking responsibility

Accountability means that when something goes wrong, there's a clear answer to the question, 'Who is responsible?' This is harder than it sounds in the context of AI, because AI systems often involve multiple parties; the model developer, the organization deploying it, the team using it, and the individuals whose decisions the AI influences.

---

[8] www.reuters.com/article/world/insight-amazon-scraps-secret-ai-recruiting-tool-that-showed-bias-against-women-idUSKCN1MK0AG/

Swedish fintech firm Klarna provides an instructive case study in the limits of AI accountability.[9] In May 2022, the company announced it would cut 700 positions, around 10 per cent of its workforce, and rely on AI chatbots to handle most customer inquiries. By 2024, CEO Sebastian Siemiatkowski boasted that the system performed the work of 700 people and that chatbots had become 'smarter than people'.

The experiment backfired. Customers complained that the automated system sent them in circles and failed to resolve problems. The Swedish Financial Supervisory Authority opened an investigation after experiencing the same issues. Siemiatkowski eventually conceded that the cost-cutting went too far, admitting in an interview that the company had become 'too dependent on automation'. Klarna has since abandoned its hiring freeze and brought back staff to its customer service team.

The problem wasn't that Klarna used AI, it's that it abdicated responsibility for customer service outcomes to the AI without maintaining adequate human oversight. When the system failed, there was no one accountable for fixing individual customer problems because there was no one in the loop. Effective accountability in AI requires:

- Clear ownership: someone specific must be responsible for AI system outcomes.
- Feedback loops: mechanisms to identify when AI systems aren't working as intended.
- Escalation paths: ways for people to reach humans when AI systems fail them.
- Post-incident reviews: learning from failures to prevent recurrence.

[9]www.klarna.com/international/press/klarna-ai-assistant-handles-two-thirds-of-customer-service-chats-in-its-first-month/

5. Sustainability: long-term thinking

Sustainability in AI has two dimensions – environmental sustainability (the energy and resource costs of AI systems) and organizational sustainability (whether your AI approach is maintainable over time).

On the environmental front, the numbers are sobering. Training large AI models requires enormous computational resources, which translates to significant energy consumption and carbon emissions. Running AI systems at scale compounds this impact. Organizations need to consider:

- whether the benefits of a particular AI application justify its environmental costs;
- how to optimize AI systems for efficiency without sacrificing effectiveness; and
- whether to use cloud services that commit to renewable energy.

PRACTICAL SUSTAINABILITY MOVES I APPLY WITH CLIENTS

- Prefer efficient models first. Start with distilled or small-context models and only step up when accuracy deltas justify it.
- Run where it's green. Choose cloud regions and providers with carbon-free energy commitments and publish your choice.
- Cache and batch. De-duplicate prompts, cache embeddings, and batch long-running jobs during off-peak energy windows.
- Track a simple KPI. 'Kg CO_2e per 1,000 requests' or 'watt-hours per task' forces hard trade-off conversations.
- Transparency by default. Publish an annual AI footprint note in sustainability reports alongside cost and quality metrics.

But organizational sustainability is equally important and often overlooked. Many AI initiatives fail not because the technology doesn't work, but because organizations can't sustain them. They require specialized expertise that's hard to retain, depend on external vendors whose priorities shift, or create technical debt that becomes unmaintainable.

Sustainable AI approaches share several characteristics:

- They build on skills your team can develop and maintain, not just buy temporarily.
- They integrate with your existing systems rather than creating isolated solutions.
- They create value consistently enough to justify ongoing investment.
- They establish patterns that scale as AI capabilities advance.

Building your AI gut instinct

These five pillars – privacy, transparency, inclusivity, accountability and sustainability – aren't meant to be a bureaucratic checklist. They're meant to become your organization's ethical instincts, the automatic reflexes that guide AI decisions even when you're moving fast.

The goal isn't to slow down AI adoption, the competitive landscape won't allow for that luxury. The goal is to develop the organizational equivalent of a reliable gut instinct that helps you navigate these decisions quickly and consistently. This means establishing clear principles before you need them, training your teams to recognize ethical red flags, and building systems that make the right choice the easy choice.

Just as your biological gut influences your brain without you consciously thinking about it, your organizational AI ethics framework should guide decisions seamlessly, helping teams implement AI solutions that amplify human capabilities while preserving human agency and dignity. The alternative – implementing AI without developing this ethical instinct – is like having a powerful brain with no gut to guide it. And we all know how that story ends, with very smart people making very stupid decisions.

Learning from both the gut-brain axis analogy and historical precedents like nuclear technology, we need to build sustainable AI habits that don't require constant willpower to maintain. Just as weight loss drugs work only as long as you take them, AI ethics frameworks work only as long as they're actively maintained and integrated into organizational culture.

The best AI implementations create positive feedback loops – they make ethical behaviour easier, not harder. They embed human judgement into systems rather than removing it. They create transparency rather than opacity. And they prepare organizations for increasingly powerful AI capabilities by establishing patterns of responsible use from the beginning.

Creating value alignment between AI systems and organizational values

Ethics frameworks matter. So does thinking carefully about where humans sit in the loop. But here's the thing – none of that works unless your AI systems actually reflect what your organization values. And that's harder than it sounds.

Most organizations haven't articulated their values with enough precision to guide real AI decisions. 'We value customer service' doesn't tell you whether to automate support or keep humans answering calls. 'We value efficiency' doesn't tell you whether to cut headcount or redeploy people to work that actually needs human judgement.

Value alignment means getting specific about trade-offs. It means answering the hard questions before you're forced to answer them implicitly through implementation choices that may not align with what leadership actually wants.

When efficiency conflicts with human judgement, which wins?
AI can make decisions faster and more consistently than humans. But human judgement catches edge cases and brings contextual understanding that AI misses. You need to know which matters more for each use case.

When cost reduction conflicts with service quality, where's the line?
AI can handle more interactions with less labour. But at some point, you're trading customer satisfaction for cost savings. What level of service are you actually committed to maintaining?

When innovation conflicts with risk mitigation, how do you balance?
Some organizations move fast and accept occasional failures. Others move deliberately and avoid being first. Neither is wrong, but you need to know which you are before you're tested.

When individual convenience conflicts with collective welfare, what takes priority?
AI can personalize experiences and optimize for individual preferences. Sometimes that comes at the expense of broader societal goods. Where do you draw the line?

These aren't abstract philosophical questions. They're practical decision points your teams will face repeatedly. If you haven't answered them in advance, your teams will answer them anyway through their implementation choices.

The organizations that build the strongest AI gut instincts do this values-clarification work upfront, then consistently reinforce those values through implementation. Over time, these values become embedded in organizational culture. They become the gut instinct that guides teams automatically, even as the technology gets more sophisticated and the decisions get more complex.

This is what we mean by building an AI gut instinct: creating organizational reflexes that automatically steer towards beneficial outcomes, even as the technology becomes more powerful and the temptations to cut corners become more seductive.

Moving forward: ethics in context

The ethical frameworks we've just explored – the five pillars, the human in the loop decisions, the value alignment work – these aren't meant to exist in isolation. They're foundational, yes. Essential, absolutely. But here's the thing: your internal AI ethics need to sit within a much wider governance landscape. One that's continually moving evolving expanding.

Think about it. While you're building your internal frameworks, industry standards are being written. Regulations are being passed. Best practices are emerging from real-world successes and, more often, failures. And all of this is happening at a pace we've never experienced before.

In Chapter 6: 'The AI seatbelt problem', we're going to zoom out and look at this broader ecosystem – the benchmarks, guidelines, codes of conduct, legislation and public education that together create what I call the multi-layered framework for AI safety. But more importantly, we'll examine what this means for you personally. Because here's what I've learned from years of helping organizations navigate this space – you can build the most sophisticated ethics framework internally, but if you don't understand how it connects to the wider regulatory environment, you will miss critical compliance requirements. You'll be blindsided by legislation you didn't see coming. You'll make decisions that seemed ethically sound in your bubble but violate emerging industry standards. And conversely – and this is equally important – you can understand every regulation on the books, memorize every compliance requirement, tick every box, and still struggle to navigate the grey areas where the law hasn't caught up yet: where the regulations are silent; where you need ethical instincts, not just legal guidance.

That's the tension we're going to explore next – how personal responsibility intersects with systemic protection. Why you need both the gut instinct we've developed in this chapter and the external guardrails we'll examine in the next. And why neither is sufficient alone. Because all the safety infrastructure in the world – all the benchmarks and guidelines and codes and laws – means absolutely nothing without individuals choosing to act responsibly. And that choice? That's down to you.

Value alignment checklist

Use this quick pass before launch and at each major iteration.

- Purpose fit: What problem are we solving and who benefits? Write it in one sentence.
- Human position: Are we in, on, or out of the loop here? Why that choice now?
- Guardrails: What must the system never do? List three hard stops and how they're enforced.
- Data ethics: What data is used, under what legal basis, and what can people opt out of?
- Transparency: How will we label AI influence and explain 'why you're seeing this' in plain English?
- Fairness: What groups could be disadvantaged? What test did we run and what changed as a result?

- Escalation: How does a user reach a human with full context in one step?
- Metrics: What are the quality, safety and CO_2e per 1,000 requests metrics we will track?
- Review rhythm: Who owns this and when is the next ethics review booked?

Key takeaways

- Your AI 'brain' needs a 'gut' to set boundaries, guide decisions and prevent misfires when stakes are high.
- Start by deciding where humans should sit for each use case – in, on or out of the loop.
- Use the five pillars – privacy, transparency, inclusivity, accountability and sustainability – to make values operational at speed.
- Value alignment is a trade-off exercise. Define where efficiency yields to judgement, cost to quality, and innovation to risk.
- Embed habits, not heroics – feedback loops, simple rules, and education build instinct you can trust under pressure.

Questions for reflection

1. For your top three AI use cases, where should humans be – in, on or out of the loop, and why?
2. Which pillar from the Trust Mark is most at risk in your current deployments, and what's the smallest fix that would meaningfully reduce that risk?

3. Where have you implicitly chosen efficiency over judgement, or cost over quality? Would you make the same trade-off again, knowing what you know now?
4. What feedback loops exist to correct AI outputs quickly, and who is accountable when they fail?
5. If a headline about your AI use appeared tomorrow, what would you want it to say? What would you change today to make that true?

6

The AI seatbelt problem

When did you last get in a car without putting your seatbelt on? You probably can't remember, right? It's automatic now. You slide in, you buckle up, you don't even think about it – unless you're getting in an Uber of course, then some AI voice shouts at you about it.

But here's the thing – it wasn't always this way. In the UK, car manufacturers were required to fit seatbelts in all new cars from 1965 onwards. Yet it took nearly two decades before wearing them became compulsory on 31 January 1983. Think about that. Nearly twenty years of having the safety equipment right there, within arm's reach, and only 40 per cent of people bothered to use it.[1] The engineering was sound. The safety benefits were proven. But we – humans being humans – just didn't do it.

What changed? Not the technology. What changed was a coordinated campaign that operated on multiple levels simultaneously. The UK government launched public service information campaigns that got increasingly hard-hitting. The famous 'Clunk Click' campaign in the 1970s showed people being thrown through windscreens. Later, the 1993 'Elephant' commercial demonstrated how an unrestrained back-seat passenger could be thrown forward with the impact of three and a half tons – basically turning you into a projectile that could kill your friends in the front seat. The 2008 'Three Crashes'

[1] www.gov.uk/government/news/thirty-years-of-seatbelt-safety

campaign got even more graphic, showing internal organ damage at just 30mph.[2] These weren't gentle suggestions. They were shocking, uncomfortable and necessary.

Meanwhile, car manufacturers standardized seatbelt designs and made them more comfortable. Regulations mandated their inclusion in all new vehicles. And finally – after thirteen failed attempts in Parliament – legislation made wearing them compulsory with real penalties for non-compliance. The results? Immediate and dramatic. Seatbelt usage jumped from 40 per cent to 90 per cent[3] pretty much overnight. Fatal injuries dropped by 29%. Serious injuries fell by 30 per cent. By 1982, before the law, 2,443 people were killed on Britain's roads. By 2016, that figure had dropped to 816 – despite having way more cars on the road. Today, over 98 per cent of drivers wear seatbelts. It's just what you do.

Here's why I'm telling you this story. We're in that dangerous middle period with AI right now. The protective mechanisms exist. The guidelines are being written. The laws are being passed. But most people haven't buckled up yet. And unlike with seatbelts, you can't see the crash coming.

This is the AI seatbelt problem. We can build the smartest systems, implement the most comprehensive regulations and pass the most well-intentioned legislation – but none of it matters if you don't take personal accountability for how you use these tools. You can put seatbelts in planes and trains and automobiles. You can put regulations in place about how fast those cars are allowed to go, what direction a plane is allowed to take off in, or what height it can fly at. But none of that stuff makes you put the seatbelt on in those situations. That's down to you. In your car. In your work. With every AI prompt you write. And we don't want to wait for the next public scandal, the next major criminal investigation, or the next Cambridge Analytica before we act.

---

[2]www.wired-gov.net/wg/wg-news-1.nsf/0/0C4D7CB420553F7A802574F600267FC2?OpenDocument
[3]www.which.co.uk/news/article/35-years-of-car-seat-belts-how-have-they-made-a-difference-agvvP5p97wYc?utm

The time to act is now, while we can still shape this technology towards human flourishing rather than just react to whatever emerges.

So, let's talk about what that actually looks like – not in abstract policy documents, but in your daily work.

The five-layer AI safety framework

Just as seatbelt safety required multiple coordinated layers working together, AI safety demands a comprehensive framework that operates at five distinct levels. Think of them as concentric circles of protection – each one essential, none sufficient on its own. And here's the crucial bit: you're not just a passive recipient of these layers. You're an active participant in making them work.

Let's walk through each one, and more importantly, let's talk about what each one means for you in your actual job.

Layer 1: AI benchmarks – testing what the models can do

Let's start with the most technical layer – the one that probably feels furthest from your daily work. AI benchmarks are how we test and measure what these foundation models are actually doing. Think of them as the crash test ratings for AI systems.

Before a car gets sold, it goes through rigorous safety testing: crash test dummies, impact resistance, airbag deployment. You've seen the videos. Benchmarks do something similar for AI – they test capabilities, safety and alignment before these systems get deployed.

Foundation model developers run extensive tests across multiple dimensions. Capability benchmarks measure what models can actually do – can they reason, understand language, generate code, apply domain-specific knowledge? Safety benchmarks probe for harmful outputs – will this thing generate misinformation, biased responses, or dangerous content? Alignment benchmarks check whether models follow human values and instructions appropriately.

Now, you might be thinking: 'That's great, but these models get tested all the time and they still mess up. What's the point?' And you'd be absolutely right to ask that. Because here's the problem – benchmarks test known risks. As AI capabilities expand, new risks emerge that existing benchmarks don't capture. It's a constant game of catch-up.

Let me give you some concrete examples of what we're actually testing:

- MMLU (Massive Multitask Language Understanding) evaluates models across fifty-seven subjects – everything from elementary maths to computer science to law. Over 15,000 multiple-choice questions ranging from easy to expert level. It's basically a comprehensive exam testing whether the model has broad knowledge and can apply it in context.
- HellaSwag tests common sense reasoning. Can the model complete sentences about physical situations in ways that make sense? Such as, if I start a sentence about someone cooking, does the model complete it with something that makes sense in the real world, or does it go off on some weird tangent that violates basic physics? When this benchmark launched in 2019, even the best models could only manage 48 per cent accuracy. Humans? 95.6 per cent. Now GPT-4 scores 95.3 per cent – which tells you how fast these things are improving.[4]
- TruthfulQA measures whether models can avoid reproducing common human misconceptions in questions such as 'Do vaccines cause autism?' or 'Is the Great Wall of China visible from space?' The model needs to give the truthful answer, not the popular but wrong

[4]www.nature.com/articles/s42254-024-00772-7

one. This is crucial because these systems are trained on internet data – which is full of myths, conspiracy theories and straight-up misinformation.

But here's the kicker. Even when models pass these benchmarks with flying colours, they still fail in real-world deployment in ways the benchmarks didn't anticipate.

Remember Google's Gemini producing historically inaccurate images of diverse Nazi soldiers in early 2025? That model had passed standard benchmarks. The problem emerged from how safety tuning interacted with historical accuracy in ways nobody had specifically tested for. The benchmark couldn't predict that particular failure mode. This is why benchmarks alone can't ensure AI safety. They're necessary – we absolutely need them – but they must be complemented by the other layers we're about to discuss.

So what does this mean for you? You might be thinking, 'I don't build AI models. Why should I care about benchmarks?' Fair question. Here's why. Understanding benchmarks helps you ask better questions when your company wants to deploy new AI systems. When your HR department introduces an AI recruitment tool, you can ask, What benchmarks did this system pass? Has it been tested for bias? What are its known failure modes? These aren't annoying questions – they're the basic due diligence you'd expect for any system that makes consequential decisions about people, in the same way that it's become commonplace for most IT teams to ask where data is being stored, or who wrote that algorithm, did it come from a Russian bot farm? These are the types of questions we've become used to in other areas of technical deployment. But in AI, people are very readily deploying tools much quicker without knowing the basics about where the model has come from and what it's capable of.

More importantly, benchmarks reveal a fundamental truth you need to internalize – even the most rigorously tested AI systems have blind spots.

Always. So when an AI tool confidently generates a response for you – a client email, a financial analysis, a medical summary – that knowledge should make you pause. The system might have scored 95 per cent on truthfulness benchmarks, but that means 5 per cent of the time it's confidently wrong. And you won't know which 5 per cent.

You remain responsible for reviewing AI outputs. Full stop. Especially in high-stakes situations. The benchmark scores don't absolve you of that responsibility – if anything, understanding their limitations makes that responsibility clearer. Think of it this way – you wouldn't skip proofreading an important document just because your colleague has a 95 per cent accuracy rate. You'd still check it. AI benchmarks are your colleague's accuracy rate – useful information, but not a substitute for your judgement.

Layer 2: AI guidelines – ethical frameworks from industry and institutions

While benchmarks test technical capabilities, guidelines establish ethical boundaries and aspirational standards for AI development and deployment. As covered in Chapter 5, the Open Voice Trust Mark framework developed with the Linux Foundation provides one such model, built around five core principles – privacy, transparency, inclusivity, accountability and sustainability.

Major technology companies have developed their own AI ethics frameworks. Microsoft, Google, Meta and others have published principles that guide their AI development, though critics note the gap between stated principles and actual practice. These corporate guidelines typically address:

- **Privacy and data protection.** How user data is collected, stored and used in AI training and operation.
- **Transparency.** Disclosure about when AI is being used and how it reaches decisions.

- **Fairness and non-discrimination.** Efforts to prevent AI systems from perpetuating or amplifying bias.
- **Accountability.** Clear ownership of AI system behaviour and outcomes.
- **Safety and security.** Protecting AI systems from misuse and ensuring robust operation.

Beyond corporate self-regulation, multi-stakeholder initiatives have emerged to create shared ethical frameworks. The Rome Call for AI Ethics, launched by the Vatican's Pontifical Academy for Life on 28 February 2020,[5] represents an ambitious effort to establish principles that transcend commercial interests and national boundaries.

The Rome Call's founding signatories included Microsoft, IBM, the Food and Agriculture Organization (FAO), and the Italian Ministry of Innovation. The initiative has since expanded significantly – the Archbishop of Canterbury signed in 2021, Cisco joined in April 2024 and Qualcomm in June 2025. In January 2023, representatives of Judaism and Islam joined the Christian signatories, making it a truly Abrahamic commitment. The initiative reached a historic milestone in July 2024 when representatives of many Eastern religions signed at a multi-faith event in Hiroshima, Japan, organized by the Vatican's RenAIssance Foundation (established by Pope Francis as the institutional vehicle for promoting the Rome Call).

The Rome Call establishes six core principles, introducing the concept of 'algorethics' – ethics for algorithms:

1. **Transparency.** AI systems must be explainable and understandable to all.

---

[5] www.romecall.org/the-call/

2 **Inclusion.** The needs of all human beings must be considered so everyone can benefit, with particular attention to the weak and underprivileged.

3 **Responsibility.** There must always be someone who takes responsibility for what a machine does – those who design and deploy AI must proceed with responsibility and transparency.

4 **Impartiality.** AI must not create or act according to bias, safeguarding fairness and human dignity.

5 **Reliability.** AI systems must be able to work reliably and be trustworthy.

6 **Security and Privacy.** AI systems must work securely and respect users' privacy.

While the Rome Call is not legally binding – it represents a voluntary moral commitment – it has influenced practical implementation. The initiative has catalysed a Global University Summit bringing together educational institutions to integrate ethical AI principles into technology curricula. Major corporations cite adherence to Rome Call principles as part of their AI ethics frameworks, and the FAO applies these principles to AI systems monitoring agricultural productivity and food security.

Similarly, faith-based organizations have developed sector-specific guidance. The Southern Baptist Convention published ethical guidance on AI in 2023,[6] and organizations like Gloo have been developing 'flourishing standards' that measure AI outputs against human wellbeing metrics derived from research on human flourishing.

The limitation of guidelines, however, is their voluntary nature. They represent aspirations and commitments but lack enforcement mechanisms.

[6]https://erlc.com/press/sbc-becomes-first-denomination-to-address-ethics-of-artificial-intelligence-and-emerging-technologies-guiding-erlc

They shape culture and set expectations, but they cannot prevent harm on their own. This is why the next layer becomes critical.

What this means for you

Guidelines like the Rome Call aren't just abstract corporate commitments – they provide a framework for personal decision-making. When you face an ethical dilemma about AI use at work, these principles offer guidance:

- **Transparency.** Should you disclose to clients when AI generated part of your deliverable? The transparency principle says yes – even when it's not legally required.
- **Inclusion.** When reviewing AI-generated candidate shortlists, are you checking whether the system might exclude qualified candidates from under-represented groups? The inclusion principle demands you ask this question.
- **Responsibility.** When something goes wrong with an AI system you deployed, do you own the outcome or blame the algorithm? The responsibility principle puts accountability squarely on human shoulders.
- **Impartiality.** Are you testing AI outputs for bias before using them in consequential decisions? The impartiality principle requires vigilance, not blind trust.

You can use these frameworks to advocate within your organization. If your company lacks clear AI ethics guidelines, pointing to widely-adopted frameworks like the Rome Call or your industry's specific guidelines gives you language and legitimacy for raising concerns. You're not being difficult – you're asking your organization to align with standards that major corporations and religious institutions have already embraced.

Layer 3: AI codes of conduct – industry-specific self-regulation

Between voluntary guidelines and mandatory legislation lies the middle ground of industry codes of conduct. These sector-specific frameworks allow industries to move faster than the legislative process while establishing enforceable standards within their domains.

Different industries face fundamentally different AI safety considerations, and codes of conduct allow domain experts to address these nuances. In healthcare, AI codes must grapple with diagnostic accuracy, patient privacy, informed consent, and the appropriate balance between AI assistance and physician judgement. In financial services, codes address algorithmic trading risks, creditworthiness assessment fairness, fraud detection accuracy and customer data protection.

In advertising and marketing – the domain where much of this book's practical experience originates – codes of conduct must address questions that generic regulation cannot answer. For example, is it okay to generate images of a celebrity for work that is never going to be seen in public? Or should we have to ask for permission for that in advance? What about commercial work when it gets out into the world? We photoshop and edit pictures of people all the time. Do we ask for their permission for every little edit? No, but when we start putting their pictures and likeness into AI models to reproduce them surely that changes the way this works.

As we see, most of the codes of conduct in industries such as advertising and marketing haven't been able to catch up yet with the way in which the technology is moving. And even by the time that you're reading this, things will have moved on further than when I wrote it.

These nuanced, context-dependent questions require industry expertise to navigate. Generic legislation cannot possibly account for the specific ethical considerations of every domain. Codes of conduct allow industries to:

- **Move quickly.** Industry bodies can develop and update codes much faster than legislative processes, keeping pace with rapid technological change.
- **Apply domain expertise.** Standards are developed by practitioners who understand the unique risks, benefits and ethical considerations of their sector.
- **Create competitive differentiation.** Organizations that adhere to rigorous codes can distinguish themselves in the marketplace, rewarding responsible AI deployment.
- **Provide regulatory cover.** Demonstrating adherence to industry codes may satisfy regulators and reduce pressure for heavy-handed legislation.

The effectiveness of codes of conduct depends on robust enforcement mechanisms. Industry bodies must be willing to sanction or expel members who violate standards, and adherence to codes must be transparently auditable. Without teeth, codes become mere virtue signalling.

What this means for you

Industry codes of conduct matter because they establish what's 'normal' in your field – and you can hold your organization accountable to these norms. If you work in healthcare and your hospital deploys an AI diagnostic tool without the safeguards outlined in medical AI codes of conduct, you have grounds to raise concerns. You are not inventing standards, you're asking for compliance with what your profession has determined is appropriate.

In your daily work, codes of conduct help you navigate grey areas. When a client asks you to do something with AI that feels ethically questionable – generate fake reviews, create deepfake content of competitors, or automate decisions without human oversight – checking your industry's code gives you clarity. Often, you'll find it explicitly addresses your situation, giving you both moral clarity and professional backing to push back.

If your industry lacks robust AI codes, consider this an opportunity. Professional associations welcome member input on developing standards. You can contribute to shaping codes that will protect not just you, but future practitioners in your field. The advertising executive who speaks up about AI-generated celebrity likenesses today might prevent entire campaigns from legal jeopardy tomorrow.

Layer 4: AI legislation – legal frameworks and societal protection

When education, guidelines and industry self-regulation prove insufficient, legislation provides the backstop. Laws establish mandatory minimum standards, create enforcement mechanisms, and provide legal recourse when AI systems cause harm. As the existing chapter notes, different regions are taking different legislative approaches, creating a patchwork of requirements that organizations must navigate.

The European Union AI Act: risk-based comprehensive regulation

The EU's AI Act represents the most comprehensive legislative approach globally. Officially entering into force on 1 August 2024, it is the world's first comprehensive legal framework on artificial intelligence. Built on a risk-based framework, it categorizes AI systems into four tiers with staggered implementation timelines.

1. Unacceptable risk (prohibited AI) AI systems that pose clear threats to safety, livelihoods, or rights are banned outright. This prohibition became enforceable on 2 February 2025 and includes:

- social scoring systems that classify people based on behaviour, socio-economic status, or personal characteristics;
- cognitive behavioural manipulation of people or vulnerable groups (such as voice-activated toys encouraging dangerous behaviour in children);
- real-time biometric identification in public spaces (with limited exceptions for law enforcement in serious cases, requiring court approval); and
- predictive policing systems that profile individuals based on inferred personality traits.

2. High risk AI systems used in critical areas face stringent requirements. These obligations become fully applicable on 2 August 2026 (with an extended transition until 2 August 2027 for AI embedded in regulated products). High-risk applications include:

- healthcare (medical devices, diagnostic tools);
- education (evaluation systems, admission decisions);
- employment (CV-scanning tools, performance evaluation);
- law enforcement and border control;
- critical infrastructure management (energy, transport, water); and
- legal interpretation and application.

Requirements for high-risk systems include comprehensive risk assessment, rigorous data governance, transparency obligations, mandatory human oversight, accuracy and robustness standards, cybersecurity measures, technical documentation, and registration in an EU database.

3. Limited risk (transparency obligations) Systems like chatbots and generative AI face transparency requirements. General-Purpose AI (GPAI) models became subject to governance obligations on 2 August 2025. These systems must:

- clearly disclose AI interaction to users;
- comply with EU copyright law;
- provide technical documentation;
- draw up summaries of training content; and
- GPAI models with 'systemic risks' (those with high computational power exceeding 10^{25} FLOPs or deemed high-impact by the Commission) face additional obligations including thorough evaluation, risk assessment and mitigation, and monitoring for emergent risks.

4. Minimal risk Most AI applications fall here with no specific requirements beyond existing laws. Examples include AI-enabled video games or spam filters.

Implementation timeline

- **1 August 2024.** AI Act enters into force; foundational rules on governance and definitions become effective.
- **2 February 2025.** Prohibition of unacceptable-risk AI systems; AI literacy obligations for providers and deployers become applicable.
- **May 2025.** Code of Practice for GPAI models released.
- **2 August 2025.** Governance rules and obligations for GPAI model providers become applicable; Member States must designate reporting authorities.
- **2 August 2026.** General applicability; high-risk AI system requirements take effect; Member States must implement regulatory sandboxes.

- **2 August 2027.** Extended deadline for high-risk AI systems embedded in regulated products.

Enforcement and penalties

The Act provisions significant fines for non-compliance, calculated based on severity:

- Up to €35 million or 7 per cent of global annual turnover for prohibited AI systems and providing false information.
- Up to €15 million or 3 per cent of global annual turnover for violations of AI Act obligations.
- Up to €7.5 million or 1.5 per cent of global annual turnover for providing incorrect information.

These penalties underscore the Act's seriousness and the EU's commitment to enforcing ethical AI development.

Training requirements

Article 4 mandates that both AI providers and deployers ensure their staff and stakeholders have sufficient AI literacy. This requirement extends beyond internal staff to all relevant actors in the AI value chain, including affected persons. Organizations must assess the technical knowledge, experience and training needs based on the context of the AI system's use.

Critics argue the Act may stifle innovation through compliance burdens that favour large companies over start-ups, create legal uncertainty through definitions that evolve more slowly than technology, and struggle to keep pace with rapidly advancing AI capabilities. The computational threshold for 'systemic risk' (10^{25} FLOPs)[7] may quickly become outdated as models grow

[7]https://artificialintelligenceact.eu/gpai-guidelines-overview/

more efficient. However, the Act establishes a comprehensive framework that other regions are studying closely, much as GDPR became a de facto global standard for data protection.

Beyond Europe: divergent approaches

Other regions have taken markedly different paths. The United States favours sector-specific regulation (FDA for medical AI, SEC for financial AI) rather than comprehensive AI legislation. This approach allows for domain expertise but creates gaps and inconsistencies. The current political climate leans towards deregulation, prioritizing innovation over proactive protection.

The United Kingdom is attempting a principles-based approach that provides flexibility while establishing expectations through sector regulators. However, the Online Safety Act contains minimal AI-specific provisions despite advocacy efforts.

China's approach prioritizes state interests and social stability, with legislation requiring AI systems to support 'socialist core values'. This represents a fundamentally different philosophical framework that raises questions about global AI governance.

This geographic fragmentation creates challenges for organizations operating internationally. They must maintain compliance with multiple, sometimes conflicting, regulatory regimes while maintaining consistent ethical standards across their operations.

What this means for you

Even if you don't work in the EU, the AI Act likely affects you. If your company serves European customers, processes European data, or deploys AI systems accessible from the EU, you're subject to these rules. This isn't theoretical – the fines are real and substantial.

More importantly, the Act's AI literacy requirement (Article 4) isn't just about your employer providing training – it's about you taking responsibility for understanding AI's capabilities and limitations in your role. When your company offers AI training, it's not optional professional development; it may be a legal compliance requirement. Your employer must ensure you understand how to use AI appropriately, but you must engage with that training seriously.

The Act's prohibition of certain AI practices protects you as a worker. If your employer wants to implement AI-based social scoring or continuous behavioural monitoring that would be banned in the EU, you can point to the Act as evidence of international consensus that such practices are unacceptable. While your specific jurisdiction might not ban them yet, the EU's leadership often pressures other regions to follow suit.

The Act's transparency requirements for AI-generated content also empower you as a communicator. If you're creating content – marketing materials, reports, client deliverables – the Act's spirit (and in Europe, its letter) demands disclosure when AI contributed substantially. This isn't about undermining AI's value – it's about honest communication with your audience.

For high-risk AI applications – if you work in recruitment, healthcare diagnostics, credit assessment, or law enforcement – the Act's requirements for human oversight, accuracy testing and documentation mean you should expect robust processes around any AI your organization deploys. If those processes don't exist, the Act gives you language to ask, 'How are we meeting high-risk AI requirements?' Your question isn't pedantic, it's pointing to compliance obligations with serious financial consequences for non-compliance.

Layer 5: AI public service information – guidance for everyday people

The final, and perhaps most crucial, layer is public education and guidance. As with seatbelt adoption, all the engineering, guidelines, codes and laws in the world cannot force behavioural change without individuals understanding both the risks and how to mitigate them.

We need better language, better education, more courses and teaching – probably through the education system in the longer term, but certainly in the short term coming from central government, from industry and from workplaces. The fundamental challenge is that AI has arrived faster than our collective ability to understand it. We're facing a literacy crisis that cuts across every sector and demographic.

Public service information must address practical questions that individuals face daily.

For general users

- Have I turned model training on or off inside ChatGPT? *(In Settings > Data Controls, look for 'Improve the model for everyone' and turn it OFF if you're discussing anything sensitive.)*
- Am I uploading data that I shouldn't be uploading? *(Your confidentiality policy applies to AI tools too. If you wouldn't email it unsecured, don't put it in a free AI tool.)*
- When should I trust AI-generated information versus seeking human expertise? *(Verify anything consequential. AI is a starting point for research, not a replacement for expert judgement.)*
- How do I recognize AI-generated content like deepfakes or synthetic media? *(Look for inconsistencies in lighting, unnatural movements, audio sync issues – but assume detection will get harder.)*

For professionals

- When is it appropriate to use AI in my work? *(Check your industry codes of conduct and company policies. When in doubt, disclose to relevant stakeholders.)*
- What are the ethical boundaries in my industry? *(Review your professional association's AI guidance. If none exists, advocate for developing one.)*

- How do I maintain quality control over AI-generated outputs? *(Always review, never just accept. You're the editor, not just the publisher of AI content.)*
- What are my legal obligations around AI use? *(Understand disclosure requirements, data protection laws, and intellectual property implications in your jurisdiction.)*

For organizations

- How do we create a culture of responsible AI use? *(Start with leadership using AI transparently and discussing both successes and failures openly.)*
- What training do employees need? *(Basic AI literacy for everyone, role-specific training for those using AI in consequential ways, and ongoing education as capabilities evolve.)*
- How do we audit and oversee AI deployments? *(Establish clear approval processes for new AI tools, document decisions, and review outcomes regularly.)*
- What policies should govern AI use in our context? *(Address data handling, disclosure requirements, quality standards, and clear escalation paths for ethical concerns.)*

For vulnerable populations

- How do I protect myself from AI-enabled scams? *(Be sceptical of urgent requests, verify through known channels, and remember that AI can clone voices and create convincing fake images.)*
- What are my rights when AI systems make decisions about me? *(In many jurisdictions, you have rights to explanation, to contest automated decisions, and to request human review.)*

- Where can I report AI harms? *(Report to relevant regulatory bodies – data protection authorities for privacy violations, consumer protection for fraudulent AI, employment tribunals for workplace AI discrimination.)*
- How do I maintain privacy in an AI-surveilled world? *(Use privacy settings in all tools, limit data sharing, read terms of service for AI products, and advocate for stronger protections.)*

Practical steps you can take this week

1. **Audit your AI tool usage.** List every AI tool you use regularly. For each one, check: Are you using a free or paid version? Is model training turned off? What data have you shared? Is it backed up elsewhere?
2. **Review one key setting.** Open ChatGPT (or your primary AI tool) and navigate to Settings > Data Controls. Turn off 'Improve the model for everyone' if you're using the paid version. For the free version, be extremely cautious about what you share.
3. **Have one conversation.** Talk to your manager or a colleague about how your team currently uses AI. Ask: Do we have any guidelines? What happens if we're uncertain about whether something is appropriate? Simply starting the conversation raises awareness.
4. **Learn one new thing.** Read your professional association's AI guidance, watch one credible video about AI safety, or complete one module of an AI literacy course. The EU AI Act requires this literacy – you might as well start building it now.
5. **Document one decision.** Next time you use AI for something significant at work, document your decision-making process. What did

you prompt? What did AI generate? What did you change? Why? This creates an audit trail and forces thoughtful engagement.

This educational layer cannot be the responsibility of technology companies alone, whose interests may not align with public wellbeing. Governments, educational institutions, civil society organizations and media all have roles to play in building AI literacy.

The historical pattern is instructive here. Calculator resistance in schools during the 1980s eventually gave way to acceptance once educators developed frameworks for appropriate use. The same transition must happen with AI, but on a compressed timeline and at vastly greater scale.

The personal accountability question

Returning to the seatbelt analogy: the law requires seatbelts in cars, regulations mandate certain safety standards, manufacturers design increasingly sophisticated systems, and public service campaigns educate drivers. But ultimately, you must choose to buckle up. Every single time you get in the car.

The same is true with AI safety. Your employer can provide tools with safety features, your industry can establish codes of conduct, governments can pass legislation. But you must choose to:

- Turn off model training in your AI tools.
- Not upload confidential client data to free tools.
- Review AI outputs rather than blindly trusting them.
- Disclose AI use when appropriate.
- Speak up when something feels ethically wrong.
- Continue learning as the technology evolves.

These aren't burdensome obligations – they're the basic hygiene of professional AI use. The question is: Will you take personal accountability for your AI safety, or will you wait until a scandal, legal action or catastrophic error forces your hand?

Why all five layers matter

Returning to the seatbelt analogy: we need the engineering testing (benchmarks), the ethical frameworks (guidelines), the industry standards (codes of conduct), the legal requirements (legislation), and the public understanding (education) – but we also need individuals to choose to act on that knowledge. None of these layers is sufficient alone:

- **Benchmarks without guidelines** create technically proficient but ethically rudderless AI systems.
- **Guidelines without codes of conduct** remain theoretical aspirations disconnected from industry practice.
- **Codes without legislation** lack teeth and allow free-riders to gain competitive advantage through irresponsible practices.
- **Legislation without education** breeds resentment and workarounds rather than genuine compliance.
- **Education without enforcement** relies entirely on voluntary action and cannot protect the vulnerable.

But here's the crucial addition. All five layers without individual accountability create elaborate safety theatre – impressive structures with no one actually using them.

The future of AI safety depends on recognizing that this is not a choice between these approaches but a commitment to all of them, working in concert. Each layer reinforces the others. Education makes people receptive to regulation. Industry codes inform legislative approaches. Legislation creates demand for education. Guidelines establish shared language for codes of conduct. Benchmarks provide evidence for all of the above. And individual action makes all of it real.

When you turn off model training in ChatGPT, you're exercising Layer 5 (public education) informed by Layer 4 (privacy legislation). When you push back on using AI in ways that violate your industry's code of conduct, you're enforcing Layer 3 while demonstrating that Layer 2 (guidelines) has teeth. When you ask what benchmarks an AI tool passed before your company deployed it, you're demanding transparency about Layer 1 while showing that you've engaged with Layer 5 (education).

You are not a passive recipient of AI safety – you are an active participant in making it work. The time for action is now – before the next Cambridge Analytica, before the next algorithmic tragedy, before we're forced to react to crisis rather than proactively building safety into our AI future. We must implement these five layers of protection while the technology is still young enough to shape towards human flourishing rather than simply adapt to whatever emerges.

The seatbelt is there. The benchmarks are being developed. The guidelines exist. The codes are being written. The laws are being passed. The education is beginning. Now it's on all of us – individually and collectively – to actually put the seatbelt on. Not next month when your company rolls out a policy. Not next year when regulations get clearer. Not after something goes wrong. Now. Today. With the next AI prompt you write, the next AI output you review, the next conversation you have with colleagues about responsible AI use. The choice is yours. Will you buckle up?

Key takeaways

- **AI safety requires five interconnected layers:** benchmarks for testing capabilities, ethical guidelines, industry-specific codes of conduct, legal regulations and public education – each necessary but insufficient alone.

- **Individual accountability is the critical missing piece:** all the safety infrastructure in the world means nothing without individuals choosing to act responsibly with AI tools in their daily work.
- **The seatbelt analogy reveals the pattern:** just as seatbelt adoption required engineering, regulation, industry standards, and public education – plus personal choice – AI safety demands the same multi-layered approach with active participation.
- **Personal action starts with simple steps:** turn off model training in AI tools, audit what data you're sharing, review outputs rather than blindly trusting them, and document your AI-assisted decisions.
- **Professional responsibility extends beyond compliance:** understanding your industry's codes of conduct, speaking up when something feels ethically wrong and continuing to learn as technology evolves are core professional obligations.
- **The time to act is now, not later:** waiting for perfect clarity, comprehensive policies, or the aftermath of a crisis means missing the opportunity to proactively shape AI's development towards human flourishing.
- **You are not a passive recipient but an active participant:** every prompt you write, every output you review and every conversation you have about responsible AI use either strengthens or weakens the entire safety framework.
- **The choice is binary and immediate:** either buckle up today with your next AI interaction or risk contributing to the next algorithmic tragedy. There is no neutral ground in AI safety.

Questions for reflection

1 Across the five layers, where is your organization most advanced in AI safety? Where are the gaps – and what's one specific action you could take to help close them?

2 On a personal level, which of the practical steps outlined could you implement this week? What's stopping you from doing them today?

3 Within your role, what industry-specific codes of conduct exist for AI use? If your field hasn't developed them yet, who could you connect with to start that conversation?

4 Looking at compliance, how is your organization balancing requirements across multiple geographic legislative frameworks? Do you know who in your organization is responsible for AI compliance?

5 For your team, what role can you play in educating colleagues, customers or the broader public about AI safety? Who could benefit from hearing what you've learned?

6 When you observe the gap between available AI safety mechanisms and actual adoption in your workplace, what prevents closing that gap? Is it awareness, resources or priorities – and which of those could you influence?

7 Most importantly, if you encounter an AI use case at work tomorrow that makes you ethically uncomfortable, what will you do? Who will you talk to? What framework will guide your decision? Have you thought this through before the moment arrives?

PART THREE

THE HANDS AND THE FEET

7

Intelligence in action

I've spent the last year working with organizations who've done everything right – at least on paper. They've built their digital twins, mapping their institutional knowledge into searchable, AI-accessible formats. They've established their ethical frameworks, creating robust review processes and governance structures. They've got the brain and the gut of their AI nervous system functioning beautifully. And yet, nothing's actually changed.

The complaint I hear most often sounds something like this: 'We've got all these AI tools now, and everyone's been through the training, but when I walk around the office, people are still doing things the old way.' Or sometimes: 'Our team keeps asking for permission to use AI for basic tasks, even though we've told them repeatedly it's fine.' Or my personal favourite: 'We've invested hundreds of thousands in this AI infrastructure, and I'm not sure anyone except the IT department actually uses it.'

Here's what I've realized: having intelligence doesn't mean you can act on it. Think about it in human terms. You can know exactly what you should do – eat better, exercise more, have that difficult conversation – and still find yourself at midnight, scrolling through your phone, eating chips. The gap between knowing and doing isn't a knowledge problem, it's an execution problem. This is where the final two elements of the AI nervous system come in: the hands and the feet.

The anatomy of action

If the brain is your organization's centralized intelligence and the gut is your ethical immune system, then the hands are your enabled workforce – the people who actually do the work – and the feet are your leadership – the ones who carry the entire system forward into an uncertain future.

The metaphor matters here. Your hands don't think independently about every action. When you reach for your coffee cup, you don't consciously calculate angles and grip pressure. Your brain sends the signal, your hands execute. But – and this is crucial – your hands have *learned* how to do this through practice. Through thousands of repetitions, through mistakes and adjustments, through muscle memory.

Similarly, your feet don't decide where you're going. But they absolutely determine *how* you get there, whether you actually arrive, and what condition you're in when you do. Bad feet, bad shoes, or an unstable foundation, and even the clearest destination becomes unreachable.

Most organizations I encounter have spent 90 per cent of their AI transformation effort on the brain – the technology, the infrastructure, the data systems. Maybe 10 per cent on the gut – the ethics, the oversight, the governance. And approximately 0 per cent on the hands and feet – the actual humans who will determine whether any of this works in practice.

Why enablement isn't training

Let me be clear about something: I'm not talking about training. Not in the traditional sense, anyway.

Most organizations approach AI adoption the way they'd approach rolling out a new software system. They create training modules. They hold workshops.

They distribute guidelines. They tick the 'change management' box and move on. Then they're genuinely puzzled when nothing changes.

Here's the problem: enablement isn't about teaching people what AI can do, it's about transforming how they understand their own work. When I train someone on PowerPoint, I'm teaching them a tool. When I enable someone to work with AI, I'm asking them to fundamentally reconsider what their job *is*. I'm asking them to:

- Stop doing tasks that gave them a sense of productivity.
- Trust a machine with work they've spent years mastering.
- Shift from producing to directing.
- Move from executor to orchestrator.
- Accept that their value no longer comes from their ability to *do* the thing, but from their judgement about *what* should be done and *how well* it's been done.

That's not a training problem, that's an identity problem.

I worked with a financial services company last year where this played out in stark relief. They'd implemented an AI system that could generate the first drafts of the quarterly reports that used to take their analysts three days to produce. The system was working perfectly – technically. The reports it generated were accurate, well-structured, and needed only light editing.

But six months after implementation, most analysts were still creating reports the old way. When we dug into why, the reason became clear – producing those reports was how these analysts demonstrated their value. It was tangible evidence of their expertise. Handing that work over to AI felt like giving up the very thing that made them valuable.

The breakthrough came when leadership helped them reframe their role. Instead of being report producers, they were becoming report architects and quality assurers. Their value wasn't in the mechanical production of analysis – it was in their judgement about what analysis mattered, their ability to spot the insights that weren't obvious, their understanding of context that no AI could replicate.

But getting to that reframe required more than a training session. It required ongoing conversation, visible leadership modelling the new approach, and explicit recognition of the new forms of value they were creating.

The leadership gap

But here's where it gets really interesting. The same executives who are puzzled by their workforce's resistance to AI are often the source of that resistance. Not because they're opposed to AI. Most of them are enthusiastic about it – at least in theory. But because they're trying to lead a transformation they don't personally understand.

I see this pattern repeatedly. A senior leader champions AI adoption. They fund the initiatives. They make the announcements. They attend the demos. But when you watch them work? They're still asking their assistant to type up their handwritten notes. Still requesting reports in the same format they've used for fifteen years. Still making decisions the same way they always have. The message this sends isn't lost on their teams: 'This AI thing is something you do, not something we do.'

The feet determine the direction. If leadership isn't walking the path themselves, why would anyone else? This isn't about technical literacy. I know plenty of technically unsophisticated leaders who've successfully led digital transformations. It's about embodiment. It's about being willing to be visibly awkward, visibly learning, visibly changing how you work.

I think about a CEO I worked with who started every executive meeting by sharing one thing he'd tried with AI that week – what worked, what didn't, what he learned. Sometimes his experiments were sophisticated. Often, they were embarrassingly basic. But by being visibly on the journey himself, he gave permission for everyone else to be on the journey too.

One week, he shared that he'd tried using ChatGPT to help him draft a difficult email to the board, but it had come out too formal and corporate-sounding, so he had to rewrite it anyway. 'I'm still figuring out when it helps and when it doesn't', he said. 'Anyone else finding that?'

What followed was the most honest conversation that executive team had ever had about their AI transformation. People admitted their struggles. They shared what was working. They asked genuine questions. The dam broke, not because the CEO had shown technical mastery, but because he'd shown vulnerability. Because here's the uncomfortable truth: your people will not transform further than you are willing to transform yourself.

What's actually at stake

There's a deeper issue here that I think most organizations are missing entirely. We're not just talking about productivity gains or efficiency improvements. We're talking about whether your organization will be *legible* to the AI-augmented economy that's emerging around us.

Consider what happens when some companies enable their hands and feet effectively while others don't:

- Company A has workers who fluidly integrate AI into their workflows, who see AI as an extension of their capabilities, who've developed judgement about when and how to deploy these tools. Their leadership makes decisions informed by AI analysis but grounded in human wisdom. They can move faster, think more creatively, and operate at a level of sophistication that wasn't possible five years ago.

- Company B has similar AI infrastructure but hasn't enabled its people. Its workers use AI occasionally, reluctantly, mostly for tasks they think are 'safe'. Its leadership talks about AI but doesn't really use it. They've invested similar amounts but aren't seeing proportional returns.

Within a few years – maybe less – these companies won't be competing in the same league anymore. It won't be because one had better AI technology, it will be because one had better AI integration.

The hands and feet aren't the 'soft' part of AI transformation. They're the essential part. The part that determines whether your AI nervous system is actually a nervous system – a living, integrated, responsive network – or just expensive technology sitting in a data centre somewhere.

Think about it in human terms again. You could have the most remarkable brain – brilliant, fast, capable of incredible insights. But if your hands don't work, if your feet won't move, that intelligence stays locked inside your skull. It doesn't translate into action. It doesn't change anything in the world.

The same is true for organizations. You can build the most sophisticated AI capabilities. You can create the most comprehensive knowledge systems. You can establish the most thoughtful ethical frameworks. But if your people – the hands that do the work, the feet that set the direction – aren't enabled to actually use all of this, then you've just built an expensive statue, not a living system.

The transition challenge

Here's the hard truth – we're in transition. Most organizations have structures built for a world where AI wasn't a factor: hierarchies designed around the assumption that information flows slowly upward and decisions flow slowly downward; role definitions that assume certain types of work require human execution; career paths that assume certain sequences of experience and skill development.

All of these assumptions are being challenged simultaneously. You can't just flip a switch and transform from the old way to the new way. You can't fire everyone and start over. You have to manage a complex transition where:

- Some people in traditional junior roles need to transition to new types of work, but you're not entirely sure what that work looks like yet.
- You're building out new capabilities while still maintaining current operations.
- You're redefining work while people are still doing that work.
- You're doing all of this while your competitors are attempting the same transformation and the technology keeps advancing.

There's no simple playbook for this. The organizations that will succeed aren't the ones with perfect plans. They're the ones that start moving, that create spaces for learning and experimentation, that enable their people to develop new capabilities while supporting them through the transition.

The path forward

In the next two chapters we're going to explore how to actually enable both the hands and the feet of your AI nervous system.

First, we'll look at the new work paradigm – how work itself is fundamentally changing when humans shift from executors to orchestrators. We'll explore the different modes of human–AI collaboration, the new capabilities that matter most, and what successful organizations are actually doing differently.

Then we'll dive into building AI-native capabilities – the practical steps for developing these new ways of working in your organization. Not theory, not platitudes, but specific approaches that work. Because here's the thing – the brain and the gut matter. They're necessary. But they're not sufficient. Without hands that can execute and feet that can walk the path, even the most sophisticated AI nervous system is just potential energy that never becomes kinetic. It's time to get moving.

Key takeaways

- Most organizations spend 90 per cent of AI effort on technology, 10 per cent on ethics and 0 per cent on actually enabling people.
- Enablement is not training – it's about transforming how people understand their own work and value.
- Leadership must embody the transformation, not just mandate it – people won't go further than leaders are willing to go themselves.
- The gap between AI haves and have-nots won't be technology – it will be integration and enablement.
- Without enabled hands and feet, even the most sophisticated AI brain and gut remain dormant potential.

Questions for reflection

1. What percentage of your AI transformation budget and effort goes to actually enabling people versus building technology?
2. Where are you asking people to fundamentally change how they work without acknowledging that identity shift?

3 As a leader, what's one way you could visibly model learning and using AI this week – including sharing what doesn't work?

4 Who in your organization is most resistant to AI adoption? What if that resistance is actually valuable information about what enablement they need?

5 If you're honest, is your organization building an AI nervous system or just expensive statues?

8

Full stack work

The first time I watched someone use one of the new AI coding tools – Cursor, specifically – I felt something shift in my understanding of what work even means.

The person wasn't a programmer. They had some basic technical literacy, sure, but they couldn't have written a functional web application from scratch if their life depended on it. Yet here they were, building a reasonably sophisticated booking system for a veterinary practice, and they were doing it by having a conversation.

'I need a homepage with our logo and opening hours', they said. The AI generated the code. Compiled it. Created a working page. They looked at it. 'Actually, make the logo bigger and add a photo of a happy dog.' The AI adjusted. They kept going. 'Now I need a booking form where people can select their pet type, the reason for the visit, and choose an available time slot.'

In about twenty minutes, they had a functional prototype that would have taken a skilled developer several hours to build from scratch. But here is what struck me: they weren't coding. They were directing. They were orchestrating. They were doing something that looked less like traditional programming and more like . . . well, more like the kind of work I do when I'm working with a talented team.

Andrej Karpathy has a term for this new way of working. He calls it 'vibe coding'.[1] While that might sound flippant, it captures something profound about what's changing. We have gone from talking to an AI and we do the work, to we talk to an AI and it does the work. Vibe working has arrived for code, and it's coming for everything else.

From instructions to vibes

Traditional programming required extreme precision. You had to tell the computer exactly what to do, in exactly the right syntax, with exactly the right logic. One misplaced semicolon, one misnamed variable, and the whole thing broke. It was like being a conductor where the orchestra only played if you hit every single note of the score perfectly.

But these new AI systems? They work more like . . . well, like working with humans. You can be somewhat vague. You can say 'make it feel more professional' or 'this needs more energy' or 'the vibe is off here'. And the system understands. It infers your intent. It fills in the gaps. It brings its own judgement about what 'professional' or 'energetic' might mean in this context. This isn't just true for coding. It's becoming true for an expanding range of knowledge work.

When I need to write a market analysis report, I can say: 'Pull data on the European electric vehicle market for the last three years. Focus on the premium segment. I'm particularly interested in how traditional automakers are responding to Tesla's market share. Structure it as an executive brief – insights up front, then supporting data.' The AI understands the vibe. It knows what an executive brief should feel like. It can infer that 'responding to' implies competitive analysis. It recognizes that 'premium segment' has specific meaning in automotive contexts.

---

[1]https://x.com/karpathy/status/1886192184808149383

I still need to review what it produces. I need to refine it. I need to add the insights that require human judgement and contextual understanding. But I'm not starting from a blank page. I'm starting from a draft that understands the genre, the structure, the tone. This is the fundamental shift – from precise instruction-giving to directional orchestration. And it changes what it means to be good at knowledge work.

Two modes of human–AI collaboration

As people and organizations figure out this new way of working, I'm seeing two distinct patterns emerge. Ethan Mollick, who's done some of the best research on this, calls them the 'Centaur' and the 'Cyborg' approaches.[2]

The names are borrowed from chess. After computers became better than humans at chess, people discovered something interesting: teams of humans plus computers could be better than either humans or computers working alone. But the best human–computer teams worked in different ways depending on the situation.

The centaur approach: division of labour

In the centaur approach, human and AI do different parts of the task, each focusing on what they do best. Think of the mythological centaur – human top half, horse bottom half. Each part maintains its distinct identity and capability. The human mind thinks and directs. The horse body provides strength and speed. In work terms, this might look like:

You do the strategic thinking first. You figure out the approach, develop the insight, identify what matters. Then you hand specific execution tasks to AI.

[2]Mollick, E. (2024) *Co-Intelligence: Living and Working with AI*. New York: Portfolio.

'I've decided we need to analyse customer sentiment across these three product categories. Here's what I care about. Go analyse the data and give me the findings.'

Or: **You do the creative ideation.** You brainstorm, sketch out concepts, develop the core ideas. Then you hand the elaboration and refinement to AI. 'Here are five campaign concepts I've sketched out. For each one, develop three variations and write the supporting copy.'

The key characteristic of centaur mode is clear division: you do this part, AI does that part. You play to each other's strengths. Centaur mode works best:

- When the task requires genuine creativity or strategic insight upfront.
- When you need to bring domain expertise or contextual understanding that AI can't access.
- When the stakes are high and you want to maintain tight control over the direction.
- When you're working in a domain where AI might not have relevant training data.

The cyborg approach: tight integration

In the cyborg approach, human and AI are tightly integrated throughout the task, working together in real-time. The cyborg metaphor is about enhancement and integration. The technology doesn't just assist you – it extends your capabilities. You're not dividing the work, you're augmenting yourself. In work terms, this might look like:

AI takes the first pass. 'Pull the data from these three systems. Use the format from last quarter's report. Create the first draft with updated figures and key changes highlighted. Flag anything that looks like an outlier.' The AI starts the work. Then you come in to review, refine, add judgement. 'Actually, we shouldn't highlight that number because I know the context behind it. Let me reframe this section because there's political sensitivity around that project.'

Or: **You work in tight iteration.** AI drafts. You edit. AI revises. You refine. AI suggests alternatives. You choose. Back and forth, back and forth, until you arrive at something neither of you could have created alone.

The key characteristic of cyborg mode is integration. You're working together throughout, each constantly building on what the other contributes. Cyborg mode works best:

- When you're working on routine or repetitive tasks where AI can handle the structure.
- When speed matters and you can't afford the overhead of doing the thinking entirely yourself first.
- When AI has access to information or capabilities you don't (data analysis, language translation, code generation).
- When the task is relatively low-risk and you can afford some iteration to get it right.

The choice matters

Here's the crucial insight. Most people and organizations don't think consciously about which mode they're using. They just . . . use AI. Sometimes it works well. Sometimes it doesn't. They can't quite articulate why. But the choice between centaur and cyborg mode is strategic. It depends on the task, the stakes, your expertise, and the AI's capabilities in that domain.

I watched this play out recently with a marketing team. They were using AI to help develop campaign concepts. Sometimes it went brilliantly. Sometimes it produced generic corporate nonsense. They couldn't figure out why the results were so inconsistent. When we dug into it, the pattern became clear. When they used centaur mode – developing their own concepts first based on deep customer insight, then using AI to elaborate and refine – the results were excellent. When they used cyborg mode – letting AI generate initial concepts and then trying to edit them into something meaningful – the results were mediocre at best. Why? Because campaign concept development requires the kind of deep customer understanding and brand intuition that AI doesn't have access to. The creative insight is the hard part. The elaboration is the easier part.

But for other tasks – like adapting approved campaigns for different channels or markets – cyborg mode worked great. Let AI take the first pass at the adaptation, then humans refine for local context and nuance.

The question isn't which mode is better, the question is: Do you recognize when to use which approach?

The full stack professional

This shift from executor to orchestrator, this need to deliberately choose between different modes of human–AI collaboration – it's creating a new type of professional. I call them 'full stack professionals'.

The term comes from software development, where a 'full stack developer' can work across the entire stack of technologies – front-end, back-end, database, infrastructure. But I'm using it more broadly. A full stack professional in the age of AI is someone who can work across multiple domains, who brings distinctly human capabilities to bear, and who can effectively orchestrate AI to handle what AI does well.

They're not ultra-specialists who know one narrow thing deeply. They're not generalists who know a little about everything. They're something in between – people with enough depth to add real value, enough breadth to connect across domains, and the ability to leverage AI to fill in the gaps.

The five core capabilities

Based on extensive work with organizations implementing AI and watching who thrives versus who struggles, I've identified five capabilities that consistently matter.

1. Leadership

Not management. Not task direction. Real leadership – the ability to make judgement calls in ambiguity, to read the room when tensions are high, to rally people around difficult decisions.

AI can inform these decisions. It can analyse options. It can even suggest approaches. But it cannot lead. It cannot make the call when there isn't a clear right answer. It cannot navigate the complex interpersonal dynamics that determine whether a decision actually gets implemented.

2. Empathy

The ability to genuinely understand what someone else is experiencing. To read between the lines. To sense what's not being said. To connect human to human in a way that builds trust and understanding.

AI can simulate empathy. Modern language models can generate responses that sound empathetic. But simulation isn't the same as understanding. When you're navigating a sensitive client situation, when you're coaching someone through a challenge, when you're building relationships that will matter five years from now – that requires real human connection.

3. Strategic thinking

The ability to see the whole system. To understand second- and third-order effects. To recognize patterns across different domains. To think several moves ahead.

AI can help with analysis. It can process more data than any human. It can identify patterns we'd miss. But strategic thinking isn't just analysis – it's synthesis. It's the ability to hold multiple contradictory truths simultaneously. It's knowing when to follow the data and when to trust your gut because you understand context the data doesn't capture.

4. Cultural fluency

The ability to navigate different contexts, to understand what's appropriate in different settings, to build bridges across different ways of thinking and working.

This matters increasingly as organizations become more global, as teams become more distributed, as we work across cultures and generations and disciplines. AI can provide information about cultural differences. It cannot navigate them with the subtlety and adaptability that situations require.

5. AI orchestration

The ability to effectively direct AI systems to achieve objectives. To know when to use which tools. To craft prompts that get results. To recognize when AI output is good versus when it's hallucinated nonsense. To combine multiple AI capabilities to solve complex problems.

This is the new capability, the one that didn't exist five years ago. And it's not just about technical skill – it's about judgement. It's about knowing when to trust AI and when to override it. When to let it take the lead and when to maintain tight control.

Building these capabilities

The challenge for organizations is that we can't just hire for these capabilities – we need to develop them. And we need to develop them at scale.

Traditional professional development focused on building deep expertise in specific domains. You became a better accountant by doing more accounting. You became a better engineer by solving more engineering problems.

But full stack capabilities develop differently. Leadership develops through experience making difficult decisions and seeing the consequences. Empathy develops through genuine human connection and reflection. Strategic thinking develops through exposure to different contexts and deliberate practice-seeing systems. Cultural fluency develops through working across boundaries and building genuine relationships.

And AI orchestration? That develops through experimentation, through having safe spaces to try things and fail, through learning from others who are figuring it out, through building the judgement that comes from seeing what works and what doesn't across many situations.

The diamond-shaped organization

This shift towards full stack professionals has implications for how organizations are structured.

Most organizations today are pyramid-shaped – lots of junior people doing routine tasks, a smaller middle layer of experienced professionals, and a tiny executive layer at the top. But in a world where AI can handle much of the routine work, where early-career people can't develop just by doing years of repetitive tasks, where the value is in orchestration and judgement rather than execution – the pyramid doesn't work anymore. Organizations are evolving towards a diamond shape:

- **Smaller bottom**: Fewer traditional entry-level roles focused on routine execution. The admin work, the data entry, the template-based production – AI is increasingly handling this.
- **Broader middle**: A much more substantial middle layer of full stack professionals who can work across domains, who bring the five capabilities we discussed, who can effectively orchestrate AI to achieve complex objectives.

- **Maintained top**: Executive leadership that provides strategic direction, makes the highest-stakes decisions, represents the organization externally.

This creates what I call the talent gap challenge – if we need fewer people doing routine entry-level work, but we still need people to develop into experienced professionals, how do early-career people actually develop?

The early career advantage

Here's something that initially surprised me but increasingly makes sense: early-career people – those in their first few years of work – are actually well-positioned to thrive in this new paradigm. Why? Because they haven't yet embedded into old ways of working. They haven't developed twenty years of muscle memory for the old approach. They're still figuring out how to be effective, so incorporating AI into their workflow from the start feels natural rather than disruptive.

Within one of my own companies where we implemented an AI-powered knowledge management system, new hires could query the system to get answers instead of hunting down mentors or reading through dozens of documents. We saw a 30 per cent faster onboarding process. But the real insight was this: the new hires didn't see it as 'AI is helping me'. They saw it as 'This is how work works'. It was just part of their workflow from day one. It was the experienced employees who had to adjust.

If you're early in your career, that's to your advantage. You get to define how you work from the ground up, incorporating these tools as native parts of your process rather than bolt-ons. But – and this is crucial – you need to actively develop the five full stack capabilities. You need to deliberately seek out opportunities to develop leadership, empathy, strategic thinking and cultural fluency. You can't just rely on AI orchestration alone. Because AI can handle the execution that previous generations of early-career professionals used to do, but it can't develop those distinctly human capabilities for you.

When organizations get this right

Let me give you an example of what success actually looks like. Morgan Stanley Wealth Management integrated AI into its workflow[3] for financial advisors. It gave advisors access to a system that could instantly retrieve information from hundreds of thousands of internal documents – research reports, market data, operational guidelines, product terms.

The results were striking – over 98 per cent of advisor teams actively use the system. Tasks that used to take hours – searching for product terms, summarizing lengthy reports – now take seconds. But here's what matters most: they didn't just give people the tool and hope for the best. They:

- invested in evaluation frameworks to understand what was working;
- refined their retrieval methods based on actual usage;
- made sure advisors understood when to trust the AI and when to verify;
- built feedback loops for continuous improvement; and
- recognized that the value wasn't in replacing advisors – it was in making them dramatically more effective.

Freed from playing document detective, advisors now spend more time on what matters – interpreting insights for clients and building relationships.

---

[3]https://ctomagazine.com/ai-in-morgan-stanley-shaping-the-future-of-financial-services

That's what success looks like. Not AI replacing humans, but humans orchestrating AI to do what they do best.

What success actually looks like

I want to be clear about something. Successful adaptation to this new paradigm doesn't mean your organization suddenly becomes perfectly efficient, or that everyone becomes an AI expert overnight, or that you eliminate all frustration and uncertainty. Success looks more like this:

- **People know which mode to use when.** Your team members can articulate when they should start with their own thinking (centaur) or when they should let AI take the first pass (cyborg). They make that choice deliberately rather than randomly.
- **Junior people are learning the right skills.** Early-career staff are developing leadership, empathy, strategic thinking and cultural fluency alongside their technical skills. They're not just doing admin work, they're learning to orchestrate AI to do the admin work while they focus on higher-order thinking.
- **Sandboxes exist for experimentation.** People have safe spaces where they can try things, fail, learn, without the risk of damaging real work. Maybe that's an AI version of a senior team member they can practice with. Maybe that's a test environment where they can experiment with complex problems without consequences.
- **The middle is growing.** You're seeing more full stack professionals who can work across domains rather than ultra-specialists who only know one narrow thing. Your organizational structure is starting to look more diamond-shaped than pyramid-shaped.

- **Leaders are modelling the behaviour.** Senior people are visibly using these tools, talking about what they're learning, sharing their failures as well as their successes. They're not just mandating that everyone else figure it out while they stick to the old ways.
- **Education is structured, not random.** You have actual programs for helping people learn. Lunch-and-learns showing real use cases. One-pagers for common tasks. Integration into onboarding. Not just 'go figure out ChatGPT on your own'.
- **Metrics are shifting.** You're measuring different things. Not just output volume, but quality. Not just speed, but judgement. Not just task completion, but orchestration capability.

That's what success looks like. Messy, iterative, imperfect, but moving in the right direction.

The vibe shift

Looking back at that moment watching someone 'vibe code' a booking system, I realize what struck me wasn't just the technology. It was recognizing that we're living through a fundamental shift in what work means.

For most of modern history, being good at knowledge work meant being good at execution. The lawyer who could draft the tightest contract. The analyst who could build the most sophisticated financial model. The writer who could produce clean, compelling prose. The marketer who could design the perfect campaign.

Execution still matters. But increasingly, the differentiator isn't 'who can do the thing best' – it's 'who can orchestrate the doing most effectively'. Who has the judgement to know what should be done? Who brings the human insight that makes the work meaningful? Who can direct AI to handle the execution while they focus on the strategy, the relationships, the decisions that require genuine wisdom?

This isn't about AI replacing humans. It's about a fundamental reconfiguration of how humans and AI work together. And that reconfiguration requires us to develop new capabilities, new ways of thinking about our work, new structures for how organizations operate.

But not everyone works the same way

Here's where it gets interesting. As I've watched hundreds of people navigate this transition to full stack work, I've noticed something. They don't all approach it the same way.

Some people naturally gravitate towards building systems and infrastructure – they see the architecture of how things fit together. Others are all about creative problem-solving – they thrive on generating novel solutions. Some are visionary directors – they excel at strategic thinking and holding the overall narrative. And others are people orchestrators – they're all about the human connections and team dynamics. And here's what matters. All four approaches are valuable. In fact, you probably need all four on your team.

The Systems Thinker builds the infrastructure that makes AI orchestration possible. The Creative Solver generates the novel approaches that AI alone would never conceive. The Visionary Director maintains strategic coherence when everyone else is lost in tactical execution. The People Orchestrator ensures the human elements actually function while all this technical transformation is happening. Take any one of those away, and you're missing something critical.

Maybe you're already nodding, recognizing which type resonates with you. Or maybe you're thinking: 'I can see aspects of myself in all of them, but I'm definitely strongest in one or two.' That's exactly right. Understanding these different archetypes – not to put yourself in a box, but to understand your natural tendencies – changes how you approach this new world of work. It changes who you need on your team. It changes how you develop people and allocate work.

We need to talk about these archetypes in more detail: about how each one orchestrates AI differently; about how you build teams that have all four represented; about what this means for hiring, development and leadership. But before we dive into those archetypes and then into the practical steps for building these capabilities in your organization, take a moment to reflect. Which of those four types feels most natural to you? Systems Thinker? Creative Solver? Visionary Director? People Orchestrator? Because once you understand not just *what* full stack work requires, but *how* different people naturally approach it, everything else becomes clearer.

In the next chapter we'll explore these four archetypes in depth – how they work, how they orchestrate AI differently, and how you can build teams that leverage all four types effectively. Then we'll get practical – the specific steps for actually developing these capabilities in your organization. Not theory, not platitudes, but specific approaches that work. Because understanding the paradigm shift is one thing. Actually navigating it – in a way that works for your specific mix of people and your specific organizational context – that's another.

Key takeaways

- Work is shifting from precise instruction-giving to directional orchestration – from coding to 'vibe coding'.
- Choose your mode deliberately – centaur (human first, then AI) or cyborg (AI first, then human), based on task and stakes.
- The full stack professional blends five capabilities – leadership, empathy, strategic thinking, cultural fluency and AI orchestration.

- Organizations are evolving from pyramid-shaped to diamond-shaped – smaller bottom, broader middle, maintained top.
- Early-career professionals have an advantage – they can build AI fluency from day one without unlearning old habits.
- Success isn't perfection – it's deliberate choice, structured learning, visible modelling and shifting metrics.

Questions for reflection

1. Think of a task you did recently. Could you articulate whether you used centaur or cyborg mode? Was it a deliberate choice?
2. Of the five full stack capabilities (leadership, empathy, strategic thinking, cultural fluency, AI orchestration), which is your strongest? Which needs the most development?
3. If you're early in your career, what opportunities can you seek out to develop the human capabilities while also building AI orchestration skills?
4. If you're leading a team which is already modelling effective AI orchestration, what can you learn from their approach?
5. What would a 'diamond-shaped' version of your team look like in twelve months? What needs to change to get there?

9

The four archetypes of a full stack worker

You've probably taken one of those personality tests before. Maybe Myers-Briggs. Maybe the Colour Wheel. Perhaps you're a high-functioning yellow with a bit of red, or an ENTJ, or an INFP.

I tend to land somewhere in that ENTJ-ESTJ range myself – very yellow on the colour wheel, which is the leader-visionary type. I live up here in the clouds most of the time, not so good at the practical details.

But what I'm interested in now isn't just your personality type. It's what type of full stack worker you are. Or could become. Because as we see jobs collapsing in on each other, as we see more professions becoming these T-shaped or even broader-shaped people who can do lots of different things, I think we're starting to see patterns emerge. Four distinct archetypes of how people work in this new paradigm.

Why this matters now

Let me be direct about something: with new AI models coming on stream, we're seeing this constant reality that we need less individual depth of expertise and more broad expertise. AI is always going to have more information, be more expert at something than any person on any given topic. But they still have to be directed by someone who is deeply informed in that area.

We've already talked about how the traditional pyramid structure is shifting to something more diamond-shaped. We've talked about how early-career roles need to be completely redesigned. But what we haven't addressed is this: within that new structure, people are naturally gravitating towards different types of full stack work. And understanding which type you are – or which type your team members are – matters enormously for how you structure work, how you develop people, and how you build teams that actually function in this AI-augmented world.

The four archetypes

The Systems Thinker

This is probably your head technical person. Someone who's able to really lean into technology. Maybe they've come from a data science or engineering background. Maybe they've been a CTO before, or worked in civil engineering, or something similar. They're very good at systems. They think really deeply. This maps quite well to that INTJ personality type – more introspective, more judging rather than feeling in how they come to their ideas. On the colour wheel, you'd think of them as very blue, very analytical.

What makes them powerful as full stack workers is this: they can see how different systems connect. They can understand the technical architecture of how AI tools integrate with existing workflows. They can spot bottlenecks and inefficiencies that others miss. And critically, they can translate between the technical realm and the human realm.

In the old world, these people would have been pigeonholed into pure technical roles. 'You're the engineer. Stay in your lane.' But in this new paradigm?

They're the ones who can design how humans and AI systems work together. They can build the infrastructure for AI orchestration. They can create the frameworks that allow everyone else to work more effectively.

The AI complements them by handling the execution of technical tasks they've architected, by running analyses they've designed, by managing data pipelines they've structured. But the systems thinking – the seeing how it all fits together – that remains deeply human.

The Creative Solver

This doesn't necessarily mean you're creative in the advertising or marketing sense. It is that you're better at seeing different ideas and choosing to do something else with them. You can take the bag of Lego bricks out and, rather than following the instructions, freely build something new.

These types tend to fall in that more yellow direction on the colour wheel. They tend to be more intuiting in their Myers-Briggs style. You might call them the design full stacker or the creative full stacker.

Now, we've done a lot of work in creative industries over the years – particularly in entertainment and advertising – pigeonholing creatives into different disciplines. You're a visual creative, so you become a designer or UX person. You're a writer, so you become a copywriter or screenwriter or poet. But here's what's changed: with the tools we have now, you don't have to be creative within a single prescribed discipline. You can do all of them. All the tools allow us to transform our work between different formats. You could be a very good writer and then take that to prompt very good visuals. Or you could think and draw creative diagrams and have AI write a script to accompany them.

This is that cyborg way of working we talked about in Chapter 8. The Creative Solver often starts with a spark of an idea, lets AI take it in unexpected directions, then applies their creative judgement to refine and shape it into something genuinely novel.

The key thing about Creative Solvers is they're comfortable with ambiguity. They don't need the answer to be clear before they start. They're willing to explore, to experiment, to see what emerges. And that's increasingly valuable when you're working with AI systems that can generate options faster than any human could.

The Visionary Director

This type is less about thinking visually like the Creative Solver might. But they do tend to think through ideas and are able to jump across different things and pin different systems together. We call this type the Visionary Director because they tend to be more directive rather than problem-solving. They're able to direct other people to solve problems. This might be more the red style on the colour wheel – very feeling, very good with people, able to match people's skills to their skill sets.

You often find people like this in HR or operations leadership roles. They're very good in that red category of things. But here's what they've traditionally struggled with: if you're very red, you're usually not very good with the data part. You're not very blue. They're opposite colours for a reason.

But one of the powerful things about the AI-augmented full stack worker is this: that red person can now rely upon AI to do the work they would otherwise not have been great at. So you might find there's now a strategic operational person who's very good with people but is now able to go deep with data in a way they couldn't have done before.

The Visionary Director excels at that centaur mode of working. They start with their human understanding – the relationships, the politics, the unspoken context – and then bring in AI to supplement with analysis, data, execution. They maintain the strategic direction while AI handles the analytical heavy lifting.

What makes them particularly valuable is their ability to see around corners. They're thinking about second- and third-order effects. They're considering how decisions will land with different stakeholders. They're maintaining cultural fluency – that deep understanding of how things actually get done in this specific context with these specific people.

The People Orchestrator

Finally, you've got the People Orchestrator. This is the person who's less about big ideas and connecting systems, but is the real people person. This is going to be the one in your organization who's always leading out on teams, often a people manager, someone very good at the human skill stuff. They also might be very good in sales because it's so heavy on interpersonal skills. They're able to make quick decisions based upon the data in front of them. And again, AI might help them with that data processing, but the human connection – that's all them.

Here's what I think we're observing: this kind of full stack professional is bringing together very human skills. And these are things AI just isn't that great at. It can't lead anything because it is not people to begin with. We don't really want to be led by AI right now. It does not have enough context to be useful at that.

But the other thing AI isn't particularly good at is empathy, feeling, strategic thinking in the human sense. It is very good at inquiry, very good at reasoning over lots of data. But so much of what we face as we lead – whether you're leading a large organization, a start-up, a community organization or a non-profit – comes down to empathy and strategy.

It's about combining the outer world context with what's going on inside your world, both personally and as a team. The People Orchestrator does this naturally. They read the room. They sense tension before it becomes conflict. They know when someone needs support versus when they need space.

And here's the other thing AI struggles with: cultural fluency in the real-time, lived sense. AI can understand a lot of data about a thing, a topic, a person. But it is not living in your organization. It doesn't operate at the speed of your team. So much of organizational data is never captured – it happens in corridors, over Zoom calls, in coffee meetings, in closed-door emails and calendar invites. The People Orchestrator has access to all of that. They live it. That's their massive advantage.

The common thread: AI orchestration

Now, here's what ties all four of these archetypes together: they all need to become skilled at AI orchestration. But – and this is crucial – each archetype orchestrates AI differently.

The Systems Thinker orchestrates AI like an architect manages contractors. They design the structure, set the specifications and let AI execute the build while they maintain oversight and integration.

The Creative Solver orchestrates AI like a jazz musician riffs with their band. They start with a theme, let AI improvize variations, then shape and refine what emerges into something coherent and original.

The Visionary Director orchestrates AI like a film director works with their crew. They hold the vision, make the key decisions, and use AI to handle the technical execution while they focus on the human elements and overall narrative.

The People Orchestrator orchestrates AI like a coach manages their team. They understand each person's (and each AI tool's) strengths, know when to bring them in, and ensure everything works together towards the shared goal.

The full stack AI orchestrator – regardless of which archetype they are – learns how to use different AI tools to get work done so they can spend more time on the top four human capabilities – leadership, empathy, strategic thinking and cultural fluency. And less time actually doing the AI orchestration itself.

Finding your archetype

So which one are you? Maybe you already know. Maybe as you've been reading this, you've been nodding along with one description more than the others. That's your starting point. But here's what I want you to consider: you're not locked into one archetype forever. In fact, the most effective full stack workers can flex between archetypes depending on what the work requires.

If you're a feeler, a sensor, a thinker – if you already know your personality type or maybe you don't – just think about the way you currently use AI to help you. Does it complement your skill set? Are you playing to your strengths or fighting against them? Maybe you feel weak in one of these areas. Are you trying to find a way of broadening yourself out? Are you thinking about how to dial yourself back up into empathy and strategy, or maybe the AI orchestration bit is what you've got down but you need to level up your leadership skills?

The point isn't to put yourself in a box. The point is to understand your natural tendencies so you can work with them, not against them. And so you can build teams that have all four archetypes represented.

Building teams around the archetypes

Because here's the thing: you probably need all four types on your team. The Systems Thinker builds the infrastructure. The Creative Solver generates novel solutions. The Visionary Director maintains strategic coherence. The People Orchestrator keeps the human elements functioning.

Take those away and you're missing something critical. You might have brilliant technology that nobody can use effectively. Or creative ideas that never get properly executed. Or a team that's technically proficient but strategically adrift. Or great systems and strategy but people who are burning out because nobody's paying attention to the human cost.

When I talk to organizations that are successfully deploying AI at scale – and I mean really successfully, not just technically implementing it but having people actually use it and generate value from it – they almost always have all four archetypes represented in leadership. Sometimes that's four different people. Sometimes it's one or two people who can flex between archetypes. But all four modes of working are present.

What this means for leadership

If you're leading a team – whether that's a small start-up team or a division of a large organization – understanding these archetypes changes how you approach several key areas.

- **Hiring**: Stop looking for narrowly defined specialists. Start looking for people who demonstrate strength in one archetype but can work across others. Ask in interviews about how they approach problems when they don't have all the answers. Listen for whether they naturally gravitate towards systems, creativity, direction or people.
- **Development**: Create learning paths that strengthen people's natural archetype while broadening their capabilities in the others. A Systems Thinker needs to develop their people skills. A People Orchestrator needs to get comfortable with data. Help them grow without trying to fundamentally change who they are.
- **Team composition**: Consciously build teams with multiple archetypes. Don't accidentally hire five Systems Thinkers and wonder why nobody can get alignment with stakeholders. Don't stack your team with People Orchestrators and then struggle to execute technically.

- **Work allocation**: Match tasks to archetypes when possible. The Systems Thinker should design your AI infrastructure. The Creative Solver should lead the brainstorm on new approaches. The Visionary Director should own the strategic roadmap. The People Orchestrator should handle the stakeholder management. Yes, everyone can do everything in a pinch, but playing to strengths creates better outcomes.
- **Communication**: Recognize that different archetypes process information differently. The Systems Thinker wants to see the architecture. The Creative Solver wants to explore possibilities. The Visionary Director wants to understand strategic implications. The People Orchestrator wants to know impact on the team. Give them all of it, but lead with what resonates for each person.

A final thought on archetypes

I've determined over these last six months as I've been writing this book – which is all about leading artificial intelligence and leading change in organizations using AI – to spend less time thinking about the technology and more time thinking about the people stuff. And that's what these archetypes are really about. Not categorizing people for the sake of it. But understanding how different humans naturally approach this new world of work so we can help everyone find their place in it. Because the technology is going to keep advancing. The capabilities are going to keep expanding. But the human element – how we think, how we work, how we lead – that's what's going to determine whether any of this actually works.

So: which archetype are you? Which does your team need more of? And what are you going to do about it?

Key takeaways

- Understanding your archetype unlocks your natural strengths – Systems Thinker, Creative Solver, Visionary Director or People Orchestrator.
- AI orchestration differs by archetype – architects manage contractors; jazz musicians riff with bands; directors guide crews; coaches develop teams.
- All four archetypes must develop AI orchestration skills whilst preserving uniquely human capabilities – leadership, empathy, strategic thinking and cultural fluency.
- Effective teams require representation from all four archetypes – missing one creates blind spots in execution, innovation, strategy or people management.
- The full stack worker spends less time on AI orchestration itself and more time on the irreplaceable human skills that AI cannot replicate.

Questions for reflection

1. Which archetype best describes your natural working style, and how are you currently using AI to complement (rather than fight against) those tendencies?
2. Looking at your immediate team, which archetypes are over-represented and which are missing? What problems does that imbalance create?
3. Where are you trying to force yourself into an archetype that doesn't fit your strengths? What would change if you leant into your natural mode instead?

4 For the archetype you identify with most strongly, which of the four human capabilities (leadership, empathy, strategic thinking, cultural fluency) needs the most development?

5 If you were hiring one person tomorrow to balance your team's archetype gaps, what would you look for in their approach to problems, not just their CV?

10

Leading full stack work

I remember sitting in a conference room in late 2023, watching a senior executive explain their AI strategy to a room full of increasingly anxious middle managers. They had slides. Lots of slides. Charts showing efficiency gains. Percentages about automation potential. A roadmap with phrases like 'phase one implementation' and 'optimization workflows'. What they didn't have was a story.

By the time they finished the presentation, the room was silent. Not the thoughtful kind of silence that follows a compelling vision. The kind of silence that precedes quiet panic and LinkedIn profile updates.

The problem wasn't that the analysis was wrong. The numbers were probably fine. The timeline might have been realistic. But they'd forgotten something fundamental about leading humans through change: data is only the foundation of a story, not the story itself. And if we're going to lead teams through the transformation that AI is bringing to our work, we need to remember that leadership, at its core, has always been about helping people navigate towards a future they cann't quite see yet.

What remains when everything changes

Here's what we know for sure – change is abundant, plentiful, unevenly distributed, and soon coming your way. Whether the timeline is five years or fifty, the transformation of how we work is happening. We've covered that ground already. But here's what else we know, and what often gets lost in breathless predictions about AI: most things won't change.

Think about what happened after the pandemic. For a moment, we were all convinced that everything would be different. Remote work forever. Digital everything. Physical offices obsolete. And then . . . we went back. Not entirely, but enough to remember why we'd created offices in the first place. We still need to feel connected to one another. We still spend at least some time together in person, even if it's not all of the time.

We still go to coffee shops. Eat at restaurants. Take our children to school (for the most part). Get on planes. Go to parties. Break bread with one another. Host barbecues in the summertime. Despite all the technological progress that social media, mobile phones, the internet, Uber and Tinder have brought us, we still predominantly spend most of our time together interacting with one another in the messy 3D reality of what it means to be a human being.

This isn't a nostalgic point about the good old days. It's a practical observation about what your role as a leader actually is – to help people navigate what changes and what doesn't, and to make sense of the space between. Because the fallibility of AI systems in the near term means we'll need human oversight for many agentic tasks. The shape of organizations may be changing – smaller, more nimble teams orchestrating their own artificial intelligences. But the thing that remains persistent is that leaders still need to be the people we can rely upon in a moment of crisis. And that starts with being able to tell a story about where we're going.

The crisis of incremental innovation

We often underplay the importance of storytelling in business. Particularly if you look at the over-reliance upon management consulting practices in years gone by, large companies have increasingly become mechanized and automated, focusing on the role that data plays.

The professional services researchers Susskind have written extensively about this pattern.[1] They identify two types of organizations:

- **The first type innovates by press release.** Small iterations. Process optimizations. Efficiency gains. Reducing labour costs. They take the tools they have and make them slightly better, slightly faster, slightly cheaper. Desktop publishing instead of typewriters. Excel instead of ledgers. AI chatbots instead of manual writing. The work remains essentially the same – just faster.
- **The second type reinvents through story.** They look beyond the next quarter. They ask not 'how do we do this faster?' but 'what if we did something entirely different?'

Think about Coca-Cola for a moment. They've existed for over a hundred years. At their core, they still bottle sugary liquid and ship it around the world in glass, plastic and metal cans. That hasn't really changed. But compare Coca-Cola today to what it first was – a medicinal product in the 1900s. You wouldn't recognize the two together. What they've successfully done is navigate change every decade or so, reinventing themselves through story. Story led by different leaders, different CEOs, different boards, different economic circumstances.

You can see the same pattern with the early machines of Apple. The first shoes of Nike. Pick your brand of choice. The ones that endure are the ones that tell new stories about who they are and what they offer.

---

[1]Susskind, R. and Susskind, D. (2015) *The Future of the Professions: How Technology Will Transform the Work of Human Experts*. Oxford: Oxford University Press.

The carpenter who bet everything on plastic

Let me tell you about a Danish carpenter named Ole Kirk Christiansen. In 1932, in the middle of the Great Depression, Christiansen was struggling. His carpentry business in the tiny town of Billund, Denmark, was failing: customers couldn't afford furniture. His wife had died, leaving him alone to raise four young sons, and he'd already survived one devastating fire that burnt his workshop to the ground in 1924.

So he did what desperate entrepreneurs do: he pivoted. He started making miniature versions of his products – tiny stepladders, little ironing boards – as design aids. And then he realized something, these miniatures could be toys.

By 1934, he'd named his company 'Lego' – a contraction of the Danish phrase 'leg godt', meaning 'play well'. For the next thirteen years, he made wooden toys. Pull-along animals, trucks, yo-yos. About forty-two different designs annually. The business survived, barely.

Then, in 1947, against the advice of everyone around him, Ole Kirk Christiansen made a decision that would change everything. He bought Denmark's first plastic injection-moulding machine. This wasn't a small investment. The machine cost 30,000 Danish Kroner – more than twice the previous year's profits. It was expensive, risky and completely alien to everything he knew. He'd spent his entire life working with wood, the smell of sawdust, the feel of grain under his hands. The familiar tools of his craft.

Plastic was foreign. Chemical. Modern in a way that probably felt uncomfortable. His sons, who were now working in the business, thought he was mad. Why abandon what they knew? Why invest in something so uncertain? But Christiansen had a vision. He'd received sample parts showing what the injection-moulding machine could do, including examples of interlocking plastic bricks from a British company called Kiddicraft. He looked at those bricks and saw something nobody else seemed to see clearly.

'If we get this right', he told his sceptical sons, 'we can sell these bricks all over the world.'

The transition was painful. The early plastic toys sold poorly. The company kept making wooden toys alongside the new plastic items just to stay afloat. By 1949, they'd developed a product called the 'Automatic Binding Brick' – a primitive version of what would become the Lego brick.

The breakthrough came from Ole Kirk's son, Godtfred. In the mid-1950s, Godtfred was talking to a department store owner who said something that reframed everything: 'What we need is not another toy, but a system of play. Something where if you buy a second set, you do not add to your toys – you multiply what's possible.'

This insight led to years of experimentation. Different configurations. Different plastics. In 1958, they finally patented the design we know today: bricks with studs on top and hollow tubes underneath, creating the perfect amount of 'clutch power' – strong enough to hold together, easy enough to pull apart. The tolerance needed to be within half a micron. Precision manufacturing at a level that wooden toys never demanded.

Ole Kirk Christiansen died in March 1958, just months before his son Godtfred would use those bricks as the foundation for the 'System of Play' that became modern Lego. He never saw his bricks become a global phenomenon. Never saw children in over a hundred countries playing with his invention. Never saw the 600 billion Lego pieces that would eventually exist, or the company that would become the world's largest toy manufacturer. But he'd told a story. A story about what might be possible if you abandoned the familiar and bet everything on a future nobody else could quite see yet. That's not process optimization. That's revolution.

Most people using AI today are doing the equivalent of what Lego would have been doing if they'd just used the injection-moulding machine to make wooden toys faster. They're using new tools to do the same work. That's the desktop publishing phase. It matters. It builds capability.

But Christiansen's injection-moulding wasn't just a faster way to carve wood. It enabled something that literally couldn't exist before – precision-manufactured interlocking plastic bricks that would work together across decades of production. Any brick made since 1955 can still connect with any brick made today. That's the level of transformation you should be asking about with AI.

Leaping past the traditional path

In 2007, most Western nations had spent decades building their financial infrastructure. You opened a bank account. You got cheques. Later, you got a credit card. Eventually, you got online banking. Then mobile banking. A slow, sequential evolution of financial services.

Meanwhile, in Kenya, only about 19 per cent of the population had access to formal banking in 2006.[2] Bank branches were scarce. ATMs were rare. For most Kenyans, particularly in rural areas, traditional banking simply wasn't accessible. High fees, geographic barriers, lack of documentation – the whole system excluded them. But 83 per cent of Kenyans had access to mobile phones.

Researchers at the UK's Department for International Development noticed something curious – Kenyans were using prepaid mobile airtime as a form of currency. If you needed to send money to family in another village, you'd buy airtime and send it to them. They'd sell it to someone else for cash. Informal. Inefficient. But it worked.

A team at Vodafone, led by Nick Hughes, saw an opportunity. What if instead of trying to build traditional banking infrastructure, they built a financial system native to the technology people already had?

---

[2]www.afi-global.org/sites/default/files/publications/afi_casestudy_mpesa_en.pdf

In March 2007, Safaricom launched M-Pesa (from 'M' for mobile and 'pesa', Swahili for money). The service was stunningly simple. Using basic text messages, you could deposit money at local agents – corner stores, petrol stations, small shops. That money would be stored on your phone's SIM card. You could then send it to anyone else with a phone, even if they didn't have a bank account. They could withdraw it at any agent location. No apps. No smartphones. No internet connection required. Just SMS.

The business plan aimed for 350,000 customers in the first year. They pushed hard and got 1.2 million. Within two years, M-Pesa had become the leading money transfer method in the country. By 2012, the equivalent of 43.5 per cent of Kenya's entire GDP was moving through M-Pesa.

Kenya did't follow the Western path from cheques to credit cards to mobile banking. It skipped three generations of financial infrastructure entirely. It went directly from informal value exchange to mobile-first digital finance. By 2014, 68 per cent of Kenyans had access to financial services – up from 25 per cent in 2006. Most of that increase was't from traditional banking, it was from mobile money.

Today, over 30 million Kenyans use M-Pesa. There are more M-Pesa agents than bank branches and ATMs combined. The platform has expanded beyond simple transfers to include savings accounts, loans, insurance and international remittances. All accessible from a basic mobile phone. This happened because someone told a different story. Not 'how do we bring traditional banking to the unbanked?' but 'what if we built financial services around the technology people already use?' That's the kind of thinking that transforms industries.

Your three horizons

So how do you develop this capacity to tell stories about change? Start by thinking in three time horizons. This framework comes originally from

McKinsey, and it is one of the few products from the big consultancies that I actually find useful for this work.

It's simple: What's going to happen now? What's going to happen next? And what's going to happen down the line?

The thirty-day horizon: what changes tomorrow

Most of us can project forward over the next few weeks because we're living it. This is where you're thinking about immediate implementation:

- Which tasks can we augment with AI this month?
- What tools do we need to learn?
- Where are the quick wins that build confidence?

This is the desktop publishing phase. You're using AI to do tasks you were already doing, just faster or better. Your team is writing with Claude instead of staring at blank pages. You're using AI to summarize meeting notes instead of spending an hour doing it manually. You're generating first drafts of presentations in minutes instead of hours.

This matters. It builds muscle. It proves value. It gets people comfortable with the technology. But it's not transformation. You're still doing the same work – just faster.

The three-year horizon: what shifts the game

This is where most people's planning actually stops, because in reality, most of us don't budget beyond the next year. Three- and five-year goals often never take shape because we're constantly reinventing them. But this middle horizon is where the interesting questions live:

- What becomes possible that wasn't possible before?
- How does our team structure change when AI can handle entire workflows?

- What skills become critical versus obsolete?
- Who are we competing with now that barriers to entry have dropped?
- What new services could we offer that we cann't offer today?

At three years, you're not asking, 'How do we do this faster?', you're asking, 'What different things can we do?'

Maybe it's like Lego did with digital. In the mid-2000s, when I was working there, the company was wrestling with a fascinating challenge: how do you bring a company built on the precision manufacturing of physical plastic bricks into the digital world?

The cultures were completely different. In physical manufacturing, you think in terms of injection-moulding machines that run millions of cycles. In digital, you think in terms of agile sprints and iterative development. One works in millimetres and microns. The other works in pixels and code. Lego could have just digitized its catalogue, made an app that showed you products. That would have been the one-year thinking. Instead, it asked different questions. What if children could design digitally and build physically? What if the digital experience extended play rather than replaced it? What if we built social networks for children to share their creations safely?

That led to products like Lego Life, a social platform that scaled to ten million users across twenty-seven countries. It led to partnerships with video game studios to create Lego games that sold millions of copies. It led to the Lego Movie franchise that grossed billions. None of that was faster manufacturing. It was asking what becomes possible when you combine physical play with digital experiences. That's three-year thinking.

The thirty-year horizon: what revolutionizes everything

This feels impossible to predict. You're probably right – trying to forecast three decades in a world of exponential change is like trying to read not just a crystal ball, but a whole bag of crystal balls jumbled in amongst one another. But here's why you need to think about it anyway – the ones who focus on this horizon become the second type of innovator. The ones who don't just optimize process but reinvent the game entirely.

Ole Kirk Christiansen bought that injection-moulding machine in 1947. He died in 1958. He never saw Lego become a household name. Never saw the billions in revenue. Never saw children in every country playing with his bricks. But his thirty-year vision – 'we can sell these bricks all over the world' – shaped every decision. It led to the obsessive focus on quality. The 'only the best is good enough' motto. The investment in precision manufacturing. The patent for the interlocking system. The commitment to making every brick compatible forever. That thirty-year thinking created a company that's thrived for ninety years.

M-Pesa's thirty-year vision wasn't about mobile payments. It was about fundamentally changing how value moves through society. Today, Kenya is the global centre of mobile money innovation: 80 per cent of the world's mobile money transactions happen in East Africa, driven primarily by Kenya. That happened because someone looked at the thirty-year horizon and asked: what if an entire economy could run on mobile phones?

Finding your injection moulding

So what's your injection moulding? What's your M-Pesa? What's your revolutionary technology? For most people using AI today, they're mostly using their computers to do the same tasks they were doing thirty years ago. The tools have completely changed, but the work remains largely similar. That's fine for the thirty-day horizon. But if you want to lead in this space, you need to be asking the thirty-year questions.

Here's the practical challenge: how do you develop your own theory of change for your organization? Start with these three questions.

1. What's actually changing in your industry?

Not generic 'AI is transforming everything' statements, but specific, observable shifts.

When Ole Kirk Christiansen looked at that injection-moulding machine, he wasn't seeing 'plastic is the future'. He was seeing: this enables precision manufacturing at a scale impossible with wood. This allows interlocking systems that wooden toys cann't achieve. This makes toys washable, colourful, durable in ways wood isn't.

When the M-Pesa team looked at mobile penetration in Kenya, they weren't seeing 'phones are popular'. They were seeing: 83 per cent of people have phones but only 19 per cent have bank accounts. SMS is universal, agent networks already exist for airtime. The infrastructure is already here – we just need to repurpose it.

What are the specific, concrete changes in your industry? Not predictions – observations. What are customers asking for that they weren't asking for two years ago? What are competitors doing differently? Where is money flowing?

2. What core human needs remain constant?

Your customers, your team, your stakeholders – they're still humans with human needs. What are those needs that won't change even as the tools change?

Lego understood that children need creative play. That hasn't changed in ninety years. What changed was how you could enable that play.

M-Pesa understood that people need to move value to family and friends, pay for goods and services, save for the future. Those needs existed before mobile phones and will exist long after. What changed was the mechanism.

What are the constant needs in your domain? Not the tools people use to meet those needs, but the underlying human requirements that persist across technological change.

3. What becomes possible at the intersection?

When you understand both what's changing and what's constant, you can start to tell stories about what becomes possible.

Ole Kirk Christiansen saw the intersection: the constant need for creative play + the changing capability of precision plastic manufacturing = a system of building blocks that could work together infinitely.

The M-Pesa team saw the intersection: the constant need to move money + the changing reality of mobile phone penetration = financial services accessible to anyone with a phone.

What's your intersection? What becomes possible when you combine the changing capabilities of AI with the unchanging needs of your customers?

The practice of vision

Let me be clear: this isn't about having all the answers. It's about being willing to point towards a horizon and say, 'I think there is something worth exploring over there. Want to come with me?'

The leaders we follow aren't the ones with perfect predictions. They're the ones who can articulate a world that is full of change happening around us, who can cast a vision of the future that we actually want to live, work and play within.

When I work with organizations on AI strategy, the first thing I do isn't ask about technology, I ask them to tell me a story. What are you trying to make possible that isn't possible today? Not 'How can we be 20 per cent more efficient?' That's fine, but it's not a story worth following. Instead: What would it mean if your team could spend a day a week on creative work instead of administrative tasks? What would change if you could offer personalized service at scale? What becomes possible if you could analyse patterns across millions of data points in real time?

Paint that picture. Make it tangible. Help people see themselves in that future. Then work backwards. If that's where we're going in three years, what needs to happen next year? And if that's next year, what do we need to start this quarter? That's how you build a roadmap that's actually a story, not just a list of deliverables.

When desktop publishing became revolution

Here's the thing about Ole Kirk Christiansen's injection-moulding machine: the first things he made with it were pretty mediocre. Early plastic toys that didn't sell well. Clunky attempts at plastic bricks that didn't quite work.

It took years to figure out the right plastic. Years to develop the interlocking system. Years to build the manufacturing precision. The revolutionary technology didn't create instant transformation. It created the possibility of transformation – which they then had to work incredibly hard to realize.

The same is true with AI in your organization. Using Claude or ChatGPT to write faster emails isn't revolution. But it might be practice. It might be building the muscle that lets you ask bigger questions later. It might be developing the comfort with AI that means when the truly transformative application emerges, your team is ready to recognize it and move on it.

M-Pesa didn't start as the dominant financial platform in East Africa. It started as a microfinance experiment in a dusty town north of Nairobi. The team had to learn what people actually wanted (money transfer, not loans). They had to figure out agent management. They had to navigate regulation. They had to convince people to trust putting money on their phones. The revolutionary potential was there. But realizing it took work, adaptation, and a willingness to keep telling the story even when it wasn't clear it would work.

A story worth following

I think about that executive in the conference room, clicking through the slides about efficiency gains. They weren't wrong about the numbers, but they forgot that data tells you what happened. Story tells you why it matters.

The job of reinvention is the job of a leader. And if you're going to lead through the AI transformation, you need to start mapping out what it might look like to bring AI into your work in the next three months, the next three years, the next thirty years. Not because you'll be right about all of it, you won't be. Ole Kirk Christiansen couldn't have predicted Legoland theme parks or billion-pound movie franchises. The M-Pesa team couldn't have predicted that Kenya would become the global epicentre of mobile money innovation. But the act of trying to see that far forces you to think beyond process optimization. It forces you to ask revolutionary questions instead of incremental ones. And when you can tell that story – when you can help your team see both what's changing and what endures, both the immediate steps and the distant horizon – that's when you're no longer just implementing tools. That's when you're actually leading.

Looking back now, I think that executive's mistake wasn't the data or the strategy, it was forgetting that humans don't follow roadmaps. We follow stories. And in a world where AI is changing how we work, the most valuable skill a leader can develop isn't technical mastery, it's the ability to tell a story about the future that makes people want to walk towards it with you.

Ole Kirk Christiansen told a story about plastic bricks that could be sold all over the world. He died before he saw it come true, but his vision shaped a company that thrived for nearly a century.

The M-Pesa team told a story about financial services accessible to anyone with a phone. They revolutionized not just Kenya's economy, but became the model for mobile money globally.

What's your story? Not your efficiency gains or your optimization metrics. Your actual story. The one about what becomes possible when you combine the unchanging needs of humans with the changing capabilities of technology. Because that is the story your team is waiting to hear. And that's the story that turns change from something we fear into something we choose to pursue together.

Key takeaways

- Leadership requires storytelling, not just data. While data provides evidence, it's the narrative that inspires action and helps teams navigate uncertainty during times of change.
- Think across three time horizons. Map your AI strategy across thirty days (practical experimentation), three years (strategic transformation), and thirty years (revolutionary thinking) to balance immediate action with long-term vision.
- Combine what's changing with what's constant. Revolutionary innovation happens at the intersection of evolving technological capabilities and unchanging human needs – like Lego's creative play or M-Pesa's value transfer.
- Revolutionary technology requires practice. The first uses of transformative technology are often mediocre. Building familiarity with AI tools today prepares your team to recognize and act on truly transformative applications tomorrow.
- Ask revolutionary questions, not just incremental ones. Instead of focusing solely on efficiency gains, ask what becomes possible when you fundamentally re-imagine how work gets done.
- Develop your theory of change. Understand what's actually changing in your industry, identify the constant human needs you serve, and explore what becomes possible at their intersection.

- Humans follow stories, not roadmaps. The most valuable leadership skill in the age of AI isn't technical mastery – it's the ability to tell a compelling story about the future that makes people want to walk towards it with you.

Questions for reflection

1. What's your thirty-day horizon? What small, practical changes could you make in the next month that would help your team build familiarity with AI tools? Don't worry about transformation yet – just focus on practice.
2. What's your three-year horizon? If AI continues developing at its current pace, what aspects of your work could fundamentally shift? What would you want to preserve, and what would you be excited to re-imagine?
3. What's your thirty-year horizon? This one's hard, but worth attempting. What constant human needs does your organization serve? How might those needs be met in entirely new ways as technology evolves?
4. What's your injection moulding? What technology or capability exists right now that you might be dismissing as 'just another tool' but could actually enable something revolutionary if you thought about it differently?
5. What's your story? If you had to explain to your team why engaging with AI matters – not just for efficiency, but for what becomes possible – what would you say? What future would you invite them to walk towards with you?
6. Who are you learning from? Which leaders, organizations or examples are demonstrating the kind of transformative thinking you want to develop? What can you learn from how they're approaching change?

Conclusion: the choice before us

About a month ago, a friend from church reached out with an unusual request. Could I speak to his sixteen-year-old son about A-levels? About what university degree he should pursue?

I've given career advice before. This felt different. The conversation was harder than I expected. Not because the young man wasn't smart – he was. Sharp, actually. Already building his own code and tools. Playing around with what I've been calling vibe-coding throughout this book. Learning computer science. Thinking about building AI. But he wasn't asking what to study. Not really.

He was asking where this is all going in five to seven years' time. By the time he finishes A-levels, completes university, comes out the other side – what kind of job is even going to be available to him?

I had to be honest with him. The exact shape of the answer isn't simple. It's not as straightforward as knowing what role is going to exist. Because here's what we do know: bits of jobs are disappearing. Not whole jobs. Bits. Researchers no longer spend hours in front of Google. Coders are not running their own tests or doing their own QA work. Recruiters are not sifting through CVs manually. These aren't whole jobs disappearing. They're parts of jobs. Tasks. The individual pieces that make up roles inside organizations.

Jobs – those tasks – will keep vanishing. But roles will continue to exist. They'll just need to be restructured. That's what made the conversation so difficult. That restructure of what roles look like is why this jagged frontier is so hard to navigate. Even in the months it's taken me to write this book, things have moved forward at what seems like a crazy fast pace in one area and glacially slow in the next. I couldn't give him a map because the terrain is still forming.

The jagged frontier

We're living through what Ethan Mollick calls the 'jagged frontier' of AI. My Instagram feed is flooded with Sora videos of friends 'cameoing' in crazy scenarios (yes Nils Smith, I am talking about you). GPT 5 launched with much fanfare and subsequent disappointment that we had not yet reached AGI, though Altman and co are still very much pushing for that aim with every podcast appearance and keynote.

Technology doesn't emerge into the world fully formed. It comes careering down the road like bulls through the streets of Pamplona, a spectacle with horns, with little regard for the people who may be in the way.

We've learned this lesson before. Cambridge Analytica. Doom scrolling. The Arab Spring. A president with an ever-available microphone. Failed attempts at the metaverse. Crypto-scammers and alt-coins. Every unintended manifestation that the technology of the 2010s and early 2020s has given us. Those who create these amazing tools rarely have the ability to govern them. Governments, regulators and industry bodies are in a constant state of catch-up, trying to both harness their power and contain their destructive tendencies.

But we also cannot ignore that the allure of technology pulls at a very real human tension.

Like a rubber band stretched between two ends: privacy and utility. A tension that has shown time and again that we will give up privacy for utility. That tension often means we have to deal with things getting worse before they get better.

We're already wrestling with the new paradigm this tension has created. Where social media gave us The Anxious Generation, one characterized by endemic anxiety brought about by smartphones and the sacrifice of personal privacy to advertising-hungry algorithms, AI presents us with the flip side of that rubber band.

Utility.

AI promises personal productivity, prosperity, potential abundance. All virtuous aims if it were just that easy. But if we do not get ahead of this, we could have another far worse outcome than AI slop filling our feeds or AI bots luring our young people into pseudo-social relationships.

We could give rise to the Useless Generation.

What we actually want

We stand at the shoreline of what feels like a vast ocean of possibility. The expansive and all-encompassing nature of AI's impact on the world can feel overwhelming.

The AI utopians like Sam Altman and Oxford's Nick Bostrom paint a picture of abundance, pleasure, time no longer being our scarcest resource. We are promised everything from three-day work weeks to home automation robots to take care of us into our old age.

The obvious side effect is that we have less work to do ourselves.

I just do not think that is what we really want.

Do we want less drudgery in our work? Sure thing. Less bureaucracy? Please. Less busy work just to keep up with the Joneses? Absolutely.

But complete automation of society and the decoupling of endeavour from achievement? I do not think so.

Work is a reality of survival and hardship for most of the world, yes. But it is also something we derive great meaning from. In my faith tradition, God gives us work to do. To go forth and multiply in the pages of Genesis. Adam asked to name the animals and as a result of the fall to toil the soil.

You do not need a spiritual motivating force to see that without work most of us feel we are missing out on something unconnected to financial reward and Maslovian fulfilment of our needs.

We work because we want to. Perhaps because we need to.

The potential elimination of this from our society is not utopia. It is the opposite.

Talk to anyone facing redundancy or being fired and you will hear story after story of folks not just being worried about a loss of income, but a loss of purpose. I've heard these stories. That sixteen-year-old asking about his future was not the first person to voice this fear. He will not be the last.

Purpose is what drives innovation. Innovation requires work. So there is no irony lost on me that those who seek to create AI as a replacement for human work are also those that spent the most on education and innovation in the past century to get us to this point.

Protecting the next generation

If we want to protect against the rise of the Useless Generation – mostly those Gen-Alphas who will follow us into the workplace in the 20thirtys, by which point we may be reaching super-intelligent AI present alongside them – then we need to start acting like it.

This is not about fearmongering. It is about responsibility. The children currently in primary school will enter a workforce where AI systems can likely outperform humans on most cognitive tasks we currently consider 'skilled work'. If we spend the next decade simply automating ourselves into efficiency while hollowing out the developmental pathways that build human capability, we will hand them a world in which they have no meaningful role to play – and no experience of ever having built one.

The risk is not that AI will take all the jobs. It is that we will sleepwalk into a future where an entire generation never learns what it feels like to struggle with a problem, to develop mastery over time, to contribute something that matters. Where work becomes something that happens around them rather than through them.

We need to start behaving like that future may be just around the corner – because it might be – and begin shaping work today to serve them tomorrow. That means being intentional about what we automate and what we protect. It means designing roles that develop human judgement, not just deploy AI outputs. It means asking not just 'what can AI do?' but 'What do humans need to become?'

That is what Full Stack Work is about.

The rewiring

We have covered a lot of ground together through these pages. We have explored how to build a bigger brain for your organization – one that captures the hard-won intelligence currently living only in conversations and in the heads of your most experienced people. We have developed the gut instinct necessary to navigate the ethical complexities AI presents – because having powerful capabilities without the wisdom to deploy them responsibly is not strength, it is recklessness. And we have examined what it means to be the hands and feet, the humans who ultimately bring all of this to life through choices we make every day.

Marshall McLuhan saw this coming, even in the 1960s. He understood that electronic technology was extending our central nervous system out into the world, changing not just what we could do but who we were becoming. AI takes this further than McLuhan could have imagined. We're not just extending our nervous systems anymore. We're rewiring them entirely.

This rewiring is happening whether we choose to participate or not. The question is not whether your organization will be transformed – it is whether you'll be an active participant in shaping what it becomes, or whether you'll wake up one day and discover the transformation happened around you while you were focused on other things.

Finding your place

Throughout this book, I've talked about two ways of working with AI: the centaur and the cyborg. The centaur who starts with human thinking and lets AI handle the execution. The cyborg who begins with AI and brings human judgement to refine the output. Neither approach is right or wrong. They're just different ways of finding your place in this new paradigm.

But there is a deeper choice underneath these working styles. It is the choice to engage at all. To stop waiting for perfect clarity that will never come. To start experimenting, failing, learning, and growing – even when it is uncomfortable, even when you are not sure you are doing it right.

My point in closing is this: we all have a choice in front of us.

This new AI nervous system is the way we need to think about rewiring our organizations and teams to be more effective. We need to build a bigger brain – capturing what it is we do as humans, allowing AI to do this work in a safe way. But we can only do that safely if we build that better gut instinct. And that means for us as individuals, team members, and particularly as leaders, we need to think about what type of constraints we are going to put in place to manage our AI systems.

But finally, the thing that matters most is us – the hands and feet out in the world. No matter how good a brain you've got, and no matter how good a gut instinct, it all comes to life when you and I choose to put this stuff into action. We need to rethink the way we do work ourselves, to choose to be a centaur or to be a cyborg, but more importantly, to be a full stack worker.

Someone built with empathy, leadership, and strategic thinking. Fluent in the culture they live in. Who knows how to orchestrate these artificial intelligences without losing what makes them distinctly human.

The organizations that thrive will not be the ones with the most advanced technology or the biggest AI budgets. They'll be the ones that learned how to think and act like a healthy nervous system: brain, gut, and hands and feet working in harmony. They'll be the ones that invested in building full stack professionals – people who understand that AI is not replacing human capability; it is demanding that we finally become fully capable humans.

The future, as the saying goes, is already here – it is just unevenly distributed. All of this work is going to come to all of us eventually. And I hope you'll take the time to think about it deeply, to engage with it fully as you go forward from here.

It is time to put AI to work.

INDEX